INFLUENCING
FOR RESULTS

Gavin Kennedy is well known as the author of *Everything is Negotiable!*, now in its third edition. He is a professor at Edinburgh Business School – home of the world's largest MBA programme – and a director of Negotiate Limited, the Edinburgh-based international consultancy.

Also by Gavin Kennedy
Everything is Negotiable!

INFLUENCING FOR RESULTS

Gavin Kennedy

(Author of Everything is Negotiable!)

RANDOM HOUSE

BUSINESS BOOKS

First published in 2000 by Random House Business Books,
Random House, 20 Vauxhall Bridge Road, London SW1V 2SA

Random House Australia (Pty) Limited
20 Alfred Street, Milsons Point,
Sydney, New South Wales 2061, Australia

Random House New Zealand Limited
18 Poland Road, Glenfield,
Auckland 10, New Zealand

Random House (Pty) Limited
Endulini, 5a Jubilee Road, Parktown 2193, South Africa

The Random House Group Limited Reg. No. 954009

Papers used by Random House are natural, recyclable products
made from wood grown in sustainable forests. The manufacturing processes
conform to the environmental regulations of the country of origin.

ISBN 0 09 941532 1

Companies, institutions and other organizations wishing to make
bulk purchases of books published by Random House should
contact their local bookstore or Random House direct:
Special Sales Director
Random House, 20 Vauxhall Bridge Road, London SW1V 2SA
Tel 020 7840 8470   Fax 020 7828 6681

www.randomhouse.co.uk
businessbooks@randomhouse.co.uk

Typeset in Adobe Garamond & Futura by
MATS, Southend-on-Sea, Essex
Printed and bound in Norway by
AIT Trondheim AS

For Patricia

Contents

Preface

Some topics from this book feature in Negotiate's 'Influencing for Results' workshop, first delivered in 1991 to project managers and administrative staff at Lothian and Edinburgh Enterprise Limited (LEEL), a member company of the Scottish Enterprise Network.

Since 1991 I have delivered 'Influencing for Results' to many commercial organisations in retail and corporate banking, wholesale and retail distribution, building and construction, and the public health and education sectors. Many of these managers claim that they have gone on to progress their influencing relationships, including relationships with people with whom previously they had difficulty in interacting at all.

People alienated by the messages of 'Influencing for Results' ignore the strikingly obvious – if you don't positively influence those whose co-operation is vital to your future, or to some goal you value, then somebody else will – and not necessarily in your best interests. These alienated people suffer from that most pervasive illusion of all, namely that decisions made by other people are based on fairness, logic and merit and, therefore, that interventions to secure their interests are not required.

Influencing for Results is written in the informal style I prefer and, judging from readers' comments on *Everything is Negotiable!* (1982) and *The New Negotiating Edge* (1998), it is also popular with busy people.

Learning is best accomplished when it is fun, and I have chosen that approach here. It's not that I am incurably flippant, or unaware of the hard work needed for academic excellence, but influencing is a practical skill.

Influencing for Results improves your ability to influence others in pursuit of the interests that you decide are worthy of your effort to 'make it happen'. You will reveal to yourself (in friendly Self-assessment Tests) your potential as an influencer.

You can change your influencing style or stick with whatever you do now. Nobody can force you to change how you influence others – though I hope you realise that if you don't influence them (somehow), they will influence you!

On cue, I confess to being influenced by many people in writing this book. Apart from the managers who have attended our workshops or who have consulted Negotiate about their influencing projects, grateful thanks go to Dr Des Bonnar, then Chief Executive at LEEL, and to Michael Divers, then Personnel Manager, LEEL, for commissioning the first workshops and to Lesley Wilson, Personnel Director at Scottish Enterprise, for supporting its dissemination over the years.

Many hundreds of influential people, including cabinet ministers, judges, advocates, tycoons, generals, air marshals, admirals, civil servants, quango bosses, professors, managers, media professionals, MPs, MSPs, city councillors, diplomats, career civil servants, miscellaneous personages from the 'great and good', and voluntary sector leaders (plus a few 'rogues and comic singers' too!) also influenced me while my ideas gestated. I learned most from those who showed me that I was influencing negatively and who showed (by their results) how to influence positively.

On this basis, I invite readers to send me their comments, whether supportive or critical, on the concepts and methods suggested in the text. 'Good reasons must, of force, give place to better', wrote Shakespeare (*Julius Caesar*, IV, iii – though, beware, Brutus, the speaker, is killed in the next Act!).

As always, my family was instrumental in ensuring that the book was completed on time.

Ex bona fide negotiari.

GAVIN KENNEDY
e-mail: gavin@neg1.demon.co.uk
Web: www.negotiate.co.uk

A NOTE ABOUT THE SELF-ASSESSMENT TESTS AND ACTIVITIES

Short Self-assessment Tests begin most chapters. Read the scenario carefully and then choose the answer you consider to be most appropriate, given the information available. As you read the chapter you may wish to reconsider your choices and you should look through them again before moving on.

My opinions of the choices are set out at the end of each chapter. They are my personal preferences and you may have cause to differ with them. You are free to question my preferences, and anybody else's, on influencing.

I believe that the views I have expressed on the answers are 'best practice' for the majority of occasions but, as every influencer knows, some people see things differently from the way we do – that is why we need to exert some powerful influence! – so I am relaxed about you disagreeing with me on occasion. In addition, there are 100 **Activities** throughout the text. These encourage you to relate the themes we discuss to your personal experiences. You already have a vast storehouse of useful experience to draw upon, though typically this experience is probably half-forgotten. Your recall of certain experiences at selected junctures prompts insights that add to your understanding. As these are personal, I do not comment on them, but do urge you not to jump over the Activities as they are integral to the work on improving your influencing.

In the Appendices, I invite you to test your knowledge of what you have read in a short (painless!) test in influencing and have it assessed by myself, should you wish. I also provide an invitation to consult me via the HELPLINE service, free to purchasers of *Influencing for Results*.

Introduction

or how to thrive in the new age of influencing

A seismic shift (there is no less dramatic word for it) began in the 1960s and affected traditional ways of managing organisations, and also, notably, the family or household. At all levels, people became less deferential, less willing to accept dictates from on high and more determined to have a say in whatever affected them and their interests.

People desire to influence their immediate colleagues, their direct bosses, people and bosses in other departments, their opposite numbers in the other organisations with whom they deal, their families, neighbours and just about anybody else with whom they come into contact.

You already influence, and are influenced, to an amazing extent but you hardly notice what's going on. Your careless remarks that incite him to bad-mouth you to others; your dismissive gestures that provoke someone to turn her back when you most need help; your ill-timed interference when discretion would have served you better; and your sarcastic comments played for laughs and for which you spend years paying, are examples of the havoc created by your unintended influencing behaviours.

ACTIVITY 1

Can you recall a 'put down' somebody inflicted on you and for which you still harbour resentment? Run through the circumstances.

Whatever your age, you probably spend more time unintentionally reducing your influence than you do intentionally enhancing it. In extreme cases, the result is the same as if you had consciously set out to destroy your ability to modify the minds of those with whom you interact. You mock other people's dreams, you impugn their motives, you enjoy their failures and you scorn their efforts, and then you wonder why you have so little influence!

Just as a poor diet, dangerous sports or wildly excessive addictions reduce your chances of living long enough to collect your pension, so self-destructive behaviours reduce your chances of achieving whatever is within your reach.

There is always the risk that events will occur, under the influence of others, that affect you in detrimental ways. Your country idyll is shattered by a new airport runway, a new road or a new housing development; your pleasant suburb is re-zoned, your city library is closed, your local sports club goes under, your taxes are hiked upwards, or your country is devastated by ethnic strife threatening terrorism and pogroms.

ACTIVITY 2

What has happened to you lately to cause you inconvenience or severe disamenity and over which you feel you had no influence?

Influencing for Results reviews how you interact with others, and shows how you might improve your ability to positively influence them. You cease to be somebody else's 'victim' when you are determined to influence what happens *before* somebody else decides for you.

Many influencing techniques have their roots in good old 'common sense' but common sense is largely disregarded in practice. Other techniques, when you first confront them, appear to be counter-intuitive. So you had best come to these pages with an open mind and not a mind-set. Adopt or adapt what suits you and jettison anything with which you feel uncomfortable.

The relevance of influencing skills became apparent to me when some young managers summarised the work they did as 'being in the business of persuading people in private and public sector organisations to do things which they otherwise were not inclined to do'. Each manager was required to galvanise the energies of various people in separate organisations to achieve a common goal, be it the reclamation of derelict land for development, the renovation of the environment to improve amenities for residents, the pump priming of new developments to encourage economic activity, or the initiation of skills enhancement programmes to make unemployed adults more attractive to inward investors.

What they needed to succeed in these projects were the skills to influence decisions, both within and outwith their organisations.

But what kind of skills?

They had no authority over those whom they must influence, they had no side-resources to 'persuade' other people to do what was wanted and they had no 'magic wands' to wave. They were, in short, at the mercy of those who could make or break their projects and who were as likely to be malign as benign towards their interests. They needed to influence people – they certainly could not force them – to contribute their time, resources and support to the projects, because this was the only way they would get co-operation.

Negotiating skills were relevant to some of their needs but not sufficient for all of them. While negotiating and influencing are related, they are also different.

In negotiating, you search for an *explicit* agreement that promises a direct exchange of what you want for what they want. Influencing is different. It is *implicit*. Influencing results in the modification, even abandonment, by somebody of ideas broadly antipathetic to your interests and the adoption of ideas broadly congruent with your interests. Failing to influence them may result in the exact opposite.

True, you can persuade somebody to modify their ideas and to behave in the ways you prefer, but even if they concur with your wishes there are no sanctions that you can impose if they do not perform in the manner you expect. This makes influencing tantalising as a social phenomenon.

Everything is implicit in the 'obligation' of the other person to deliver what you expect. As there is no contract, verbal or written, and often no explicit acknowledgement that they have a commitment to behave in a specific manner, there is much room for ambiguities of intention and a consequent high risk of disappointment when the expected does not happen.

Influence, much like power, is felt rather than seen.

If you do not influence events it is certain that others will. In the absence of your ability to exert influence, others do so. Influence or be influenced! That is the iron law of Influencing. Modify their minds or have yours modified by others. There is no escape from influence, except in total and permanent isolation. Humans, anyway, are social animals. So influencing skills are always bound to be a social activity.

Weary workers say there is 'no peace for the wicked'. In *Influencing for Results*, there is 'no peace for those without influence'. Influencing skills are not just an interesting option. They are mandatory. And because everybody can be influenced, everybody *is* influenced.

The only choice you have is whether to forgo the opportunity to influence those whose actions influence you. Your choice boils down to whether you accept that the influence of others on you is benign to your interests.

Influencing for Results is a thoroughly practical, not a theoretical, book. The influencing methods I outline are the methods that have been applied where it matters – in influencing other people in real organisations in the real world.

There are two distinct approaches to learning about influencing skills.

The first approach is the study of how people in powerful positions in organisations – corporations, political parties, government offices, inter-governmental agencies and suchlike – use their power to influence those with whom they interact, both formally and informally. One of the best exponents of this approach is Jeffrey Pfeffer in his *Managing with Power: politics and influence in organisations*, Harvard Business School Press, 1992. In fact, his title, *Managing with Power*, highlights the basic difference between the two approaches.

Pfeffer, and others in this genre, write as observers of how powerful men and women behave, how they acquired power, what they do with it, and (sometimes) how they lose it. They are backed by a formidable body of research plus a rich field of commentary, biography and autobiography.

The second approach, and the one I have chosen here, can be summed up by rewriting Pfeffer's title as 'managing *without* power', or better still, 'how to influence with *neither* power *nor* authority'.

Influencing for Results is not a study of how already powerful men and women in the prime of their careers exercise influence over others. It is about that often long period *before* some men and women achieve the positions from which they can exercise their considerable influence.

In my mind's eye, I see you as at the beginning or at the very early stages of your managerial career; for that reason you are more likely to benefit in a practical sense from following the second approach than the first (though it is inevitable that I trespass occasionally into Pfeffer's territory for illustrative purposes).

In addition, by using the methods of *Influencing for Results* in the context of the world of a relatively new (though ambitious) manager, you will benefit more than if you remain in awe of the behaviours of people in worlds you have not yet experienced (and never will unless you acquire some influence or win the lottery).

These influencing methods are applicable to your present world rather than being insights into the worlds to which you are heading.

So, Chapters 1 through 16 are about influencing *without* power. Chapter 17 is a short summary of influencing *with* power, and it is included solely for completion. It is less comprehensive than the earlier chapters but it helps to put the recommended influencing methods into context for when you acquire more power.

Influencing techniques are appropriate no matter who is the target of your influencing strategy. I give examples to illustrate the different ways you can play the same shots in different circumstances. *Influencing for Results* discusses influencing for major stakes like those involving career decisions, and for minor stakes like who sits next to you at a business lunch. Everyday domestic influencing situations are used as examples on the grounds that they are often revealing when applied to other contexts. You could be a major influencer, for example, who is unable to influence those in your own home. Fine, as long as you are content with this but if not you could benefit from doing something about it (not that I seek to induce domestic disharmony!).

Conversely, you may exert enormous influence within your family and hardly any at all beyond your front door. Again, fine, as long as you don't mind somebody else gaining the promotion, a bigger budget, the go-ahead for their (inferior) project, time off for their phoney 'good behaviour', or more than their 'fair' share of some other scarce resource that you sought for your (deserving) self. This usually happens because in your wilful absence somebody else influenced the decision-makers and you didn't.

ACTIVITY 3

When did something like this happen to you? How did you feel when what you expected – because you 'deserved' it – didn't happen?

Influencing for Results is full of foghorn messages that enable you to reduce the incidence of losing out to other people's influence. You will not be asked to do anything with which you feel uncomfortable. You choose the extent to which you pursue your own interests.

I do not want to imply by this that there is something unscrupulous or devious about influencing. There is not. As you will realise long before you complete *Influencing for Results*, unscrupulous deviousness is an ineffective way to influence others.

Indeed, in the Age of Influencing there is one great law: you help yourself best by helping others, because the surest way to serve your own interests is to serve the interests of those who are able to serve yours.

Now that ain't so bad as a behavioural code for influencing, is it?

SELF-ASSESSMENT TEST 1

1. A paedophile has served his sentence and you are desperately concerned about the plight of young children who may be exposed to his attentions. You secure an interview with the Chief Constable but, on approaching the building in time for your meeting, you are redirected by traffic wardens into a new one-way system causing you to be ten minutes late. When you get there, you find the Chief Constable has departed to another appointment, leaving you stranded without a commitment for another meeting. More, the functionary tells you that the Chief Constable's other appointment is a social event celebrating somebody's birthday. Do you:
   (a) fume visibly at this news and complain that 'it is out of order to be treated this way by a public servant'?
   (b) ask for another appointment?
   (c) demand that the Chief Constable is notified of your arrival and that he leaves the party and sees you?

2. You are waiting in an airport lounge in Kuwait and an Arab male passes you, followed by an Arab woman with a leather mask covering her face. A man next to you comments on this procession as 'typical of the Kuwaitis' barbaric customs' and proceeds to expand on his views to you and some other Europeans sitting close by. Do you:
   (a) smile and say nothing in reply?
   (b) turn away and look for somewhere else to sit?
   (c) shrug your shoulders and say 'it's none of our business'?

3. You are visiting the public affairs department of a large business organisation to see if they will support your company's campaign to have Manchester awarded the

European Cup Finals in 2016. The person you have come to see tells you that, personally, she doesn't watch football, which happens to be true of you too. Do you:
(a) tell her that you don't watch football either?
(b) tell her that the event in 2016 is about the image of Manchester, not football?

CHAPTER 1

What must influencers avoid?

or how to avoid traps for fools

What habit must an influencer avoid? At our influencing workshops we usually hear things like:

'Provoking enemies'
'Insulting other people'
'A pompous image'
'Arrogance'

Now, these suggestions are OK as far as they go. They recognise, at least, that influencing is not helped by irritating other people.

What then must an influencer avoid?:

EXPRESSING AN OPINION

'This is some joke surely? How can influencers possibly fail to express their opinions? Surely everybody expresses opinions about something?'

These and similar responses are typical of people who discover that influencing is not all sweetness and light – it can be controversial.

Sceptics, who react too quickly, usually assert that everybody expresses opinions, i.e. beliefs not supported by facts. People, surely, have a licence to express their opinions on any subject at

1

any time to anybody: it's called free speech? But freedom of speech does not mean it is compulsory for you to speak – you are free to speak or not, as suits your inclinations.

And, because expressing opinions is the main source of not having influence, the more times you express your opinions the less influence you have.

It's as simple a trade-off as that.

ACTIVITY 4

Do you hold strong opinions on anything? How often do you speak about these strong opinions? Are these opinions of yours well known to those who know you?

So why express an opinion? That everybody you know expresses opinions is unchallenged, but I'll wager that they don't express the *same* opinions. So remember, expressing opinions brings you into conflict with others and you are less likely to influence them in a conflict.

At this point in our workshops, an over-excited sceptic usually jumps in and claims a *gotcha*: 'If the purpose of influencing is to change the opinions of others, how can we do so if we don't express our opinions?' With this they sit back and smirk all the way to the tea break.

But hold on.

How does expressing an opinion induce somebody of a different opinion to change hers? It doesn't, of course, and if influencing was solely about changing other people's opinions your ambitions would still outrun your resources.

In practice, observation and experience suggest that expressing opinions is a major impediment to changing the opinions of other people. You can regard influencing as a series of fruitless arguments over differing opinions, or as a strategy to modify the minds of others.

Anybody can have an argument, but nobody can win one. However, you can avoid trying to win arguments by expressing your opinions. Influencing is not about 'winning' arguments.

NO OPINIONS HERE

A state official, when questioned by reporters about the method by which capital punishment is carried out in Texas, said that death by lethal injection was 'painless'. When asked whether it was 'humane' to execute convicted murderers in this manner, he replied: 'No, I am not going to get drawn into giving you opinions. I am here to state the facts, not my opinions. I have nothing to say about opinions. Only that execution by injection is painless.'

Let me illustrate how expressing opinions unwittingly has negative consequences by recounting what happened to Anne McTavish.

Mrs McTavish was hired as a PR consultant to AMP ('Always Make Profits') Ltd, a property developer, which had appealed against the rejection of its multimillion-pound development proposal for its town centre site and was paying for a PR campaign to reverse the decision.

AMP's site had become available when the local football club quit for a brand new stadium on the edge of town. While the previous city council was delighted with AMP's plans, everything changed after the elections, when the 'Tails Faction' defeated the 'Heads Faction', who were all members of the party that ran the council (the 'politics' of the factions that run this part of Scotland is much like the sex life of a rhinoceros – only of interest to another rhinoceros!).

The new council leaders opposed AMP's development plans. They favoured 'High Street' shopping precincts built in a traditional style. AMP's development was neither traditional nor elegantly modern – it was in the architectural style hated by Prince Charles.

Anne McTavish's job was to counter prejudice against the development. Her client regarded the planners' decision with horror because it would delay the start of construction. Anne was familiar with the *ancien régime* that had run the council for years and she had mixed with them socially as well as professionally (several of them had been guests on her yacht, the *Isabella*, which she sailed with her husband, Angus). Anne was stunned when the electoral tumbrels carted her 'friends' off to the political wilderness.

Anne's problem is her strong opinions. And like lots of people with strong opinions, she is also generous in sharing them. 'How could the voters be so stupid?' opined Anne to anybody who listened (and many who listened must have been among the same 'stupid' voters). Anne didn't care about sharing her opinions because she wasn't running for the city council and she doesn't think much of those who do. 'Creeps and crooks the lot of them,' she is wont to declare, which never, of course, prevents her creeping round the same 'crooks' when it is to a client's advantage.

In the weeks before AMP's appeal, Anne sought opportunities to influence people, and I have selected a small incident to illustrate the high price she paid for spouting her opinions.

One rainswept Monday she found her usual parking space, near the side entrance to the council offices, roped off. A notice hanging from the rope announced that parking there was now reserved for 'Elected Councillors and Disabled Drivers only'. As she was neither, she was forced to park 700 metres away and then to walk back to the side entrance in the rain, along a windy potholed road.

This did not best please her and she arrived at the door looking very wet – her mascara was running, her hair was slightly bedraggled and she had soaked her left foot in a deep puddle. She hardly had time to tidy herself before her first appointment.

She was even less pleased when Hector, the doorkeeper, told her that her unofficial car parking space had been redesignated by 'Councillor Mrs Herbison', who was the new member for Millarhill, a suburb famous for women of a certain age and disposition who, allegedly, wore 'fur coats and nae knickers' yet had pretensions to social superiority.

'Typical!' Anne told Hector, shaking her head. 'We pay taxes and the likes of Herbison spend our money on parking places for people who ride around in subsidised vehicles.'

Hector nodded, as if in agreement with her sentiments. Later that day, having mulled over what she said, he repeated Anne McTavish's opinions to Mrs Herbison while she was waiting for a lift.

Hector was particularly incensed by Anne's remark, because he knew all about the penalty of immobility. His wife had not walked for ten years, since she had been seriously injured in a road accident (while she was drink driving). She now drove a specially adapted three-wheeler runabout. Its so-called 'subsidy' was a small tax allowance, which only applied if you earned enough to pay tax (which she didn't) and, like most disabled owners, she bought her special car at its full price.

Mrs Herbison snorted angrily at Anne's prejudiced opinions, but said nothing as she was already ten minutes late for a planning sub-committee meeting (where AMP's appeal was item 8). When AMP's appeal came up, Mrs Herbison successfully moved for a 'continuation' (council speak for deliberately delaying a decision). Mrs Herbison attacked AMP's 'outrageous attitudes to the most vulnerable people in today's society' and announced that she would report her concerns to the full council.

In short, the AMP appeal became a controversial issue of Political Correctness. And there is nothing politicians like better than to oppose controversial proposals with outbursts of moral indignation.

ACTIVITY 5

When was the last time that you committed a *faux pas* by making a remark about something or someone?

Now, I do not know what the 'truth' was because I only heard

Anne's version of events over dinner to celebrate her husband's election as Commodore of their sailing club. Anne was adamant that her words had been twisted out of all recognition. She had not been referring, she insisted, to disabled drivers ('Good God, my mother is disabled!'). Her remarks, she said, had been directed at politicians and their large subsidised cars, provided at public expense by the council, not the little three-wheelers ('tin cans powered by lawnmower engines') which she knew that disabled people had to buy for themselves.

'It wasn't the designation of the parking spaces for the disabled that was so annoying,' Anne tearfully whined; 'it was that hypocritical Herbison roping off the area for her subsidised car and making out she was doing it for the disabled.'

But the damage was done. True, the AMP appeal was not yet dead in the water – just slightly waterlogged, perhaps – and, hopefully, the momentum would eventually start up again.

Anne, meanwhile, was abandoned by her client. She was under pressure too to step aside and her boss had uttered the killer overtures to her southward slide in the hierarchy: 'special projects', 'new challenges' and 'take your time to think it over' (i.e. resign by lunchtime).

Domestically, it was also unfortunate that the 'disabled insult' row blew up in the same week that Angus had achieved his crowning delight at becoming Club Commodore. He was manic high, though naturally sympathetic to Anne's plight, while she felt depressively low and bitterly angry at being unfairly pilloried by Herbison.

Our celebration dinner became a wake to Anne's PR career. By the time we got to the mints, everybody was depressed.

The root of Anne's problem lies at the heart of influencing. Whatever the merits of Anne's opinion of politicians subsidising their lifestyle at public expense, expressing it was positively lethal to her interests.

When you express opinions you deliver hostages to fortune into the hands of anybody listening who wants to destroy your influence.

It may be comforting that 'the truth will eventually prevail', but by the time it prevails it is too late to repair the damage that the lies, damned lies and their versions of your opinions do to your influence. No. What is required is the pre-emptive 'remedy' of not expressing opinions in the first place. What you don't give away you can't have thrown back in your face, or cast before the gullible minds of others.

Kipling's admonition to 'bear to hear the truth you've spoken, twisted by knaves to make a trap for fools' assumes that your opinions are truthful. If knaves twisting the truth are a heavy burden to bear, they twist the knife because you, not the knave, exposed your own back. The best way to protect yourself from such knavish tricks is to avoid succumbing to the intemperate urge to share your opinions with others. These are burdens you can well do without.

If you are still sceptical, don't take my word for it. Just ask Anne McTavish what she thinks!

ANSWERS TO SELF-ASSESSMENT TEST 1

1. (a) But what good does this do?
   (b) Yes.
   (c) Oh dear. Probably your worst choice.

2. (a) Might indicate you agree with his observations if you smile. It is better not to innocently cause offence to any Kuwaitis observing the scene and hearing the man's comments.
   (b) Yes. Opinions like his could get you into trouble. If you're abroad on business it is best not to mix critical social comment with your business.
   (c) Not quite, because by expressing a contrary opinion you are still at risk if the man you are speaking to is in a position to harm your interests. As you don't know for

sure, it's best not to have opinions because then you can't offend anybody by expressing them.

3 (a) No, because football is not the purpose of your visit.

(b) Much better because it's what the event does for her organisation that counts, not the medium through which these gains are achieved.

SELF-ASSESSMENT TEST 2

1. You are a relatively new member of a five-person sub-committee charged with sifting through applications for financial support from a fund-granting body aiming to promote the arts. For the next meeting in a week's time, eleven applications have been received, three of which you wish to support, and one of which you are absolutely against. Towards the remainder you are neutral. Do you:
   (a) thoroughly prepare cases for supporting the three applications of which you approve?
   (b) thoroughly prepare a case against the one application of which you disapprove?
   (c) do both (a) and (b)?
   (d) call on the other four sub-committee members before the meeting and ask them how they feel towards the applications?

2. You have been told by a senior colleague that the vice-chairman of the committee you have just joined is usually antagonistic to your company's proposals on environmental issues. With a second meeting due this Friday, you have not yet met this person. He lives and works out of town. Do you:
   (a) wait until the meeting to make your own judgement about his degree of hostility?
   (b) call him on the telephone and initiate a discussion on his policies?
   (c) drive out of town to have a face-to-face meeting with him about the work of the committee?

3. You attend a social gathering and find that you don't know any of the people who have turned up. Do you?
   (a) introduce yourself to the person(s) next to you?

(b) wait for the host to introduce you to people whom you don't know?

(c) keep a low profile and wait for other people to speak to you?

CHAPTER 2

It don't take much to keep in touch

or why three showers are better than one

The world is full of people who know how to change the world and their place in it. You meet them everywhere. They have clear notions of what is wrong with the world and what must be done to put it right. And they are pretty sure about what is stopping anything changing – except for the worse. It's usually all the fault of *Them* (the people who currently are in charge).

'We are lions led by donkeys,' they bray. 'If only they would drop this or that policy, or had promoted the really competent (i.e. me), we would never have got into the mess we are in.'

How true!

And how safe it is to say so because it is extremely unlikely that these assertions will be tested. And what can't be tested is immune to rebuttal. That's why, while many people claim to know how to improve the world, few do it. (Arguably, of those who do, most make as big a mess as those before them!)

Now, it's not an awesome conspiracy that prevents would-be reformers from practising what they preach. No. The real reason is more stark. It is, to be frank, their idleness.

They know what they would do but they make no effort to do it. To have a go at implementing their solutions means exerting themselves. But this is often beyond them on two counts: firstly, their lethargy, and secondly, the risk to their credibility.

Recently, I was discussing performance pay for professorial

11

staff at a south of England business school with its Dean. One of my suggestions was to take £10,000 from their salary and award it only if they published a book that year in their specialist subject. The Dean objected because 'all a professor has to do is write a book' which, he opined, 'most of them would do at the drop of a hat, especially one with £10,000 in it'.

As the aim of the incentive scheme was to get professors to publish, I was not fazed by this objection. But, because few (tenured) professors make the effort to write books (yes, there is a connection), I doubted that 'most of them' would expend the energy necessary to do so, certainly not at the drop of a hat. Those professors who did, however, would enjoy receiving £10,000 and the business school would save £10,000 from the salaries of the rest.

ACTIVITY 6

In your line of endeavour, what is the one project you could do that you have not done yet but, if you did complete it, your prospects would be enhanced?

Many people you meet are quite capable of writing a book (or running their own business, or standing for public office, or completing appropriate tasks in their line of work), but almost all of them never put their fingers to a word processor (or its equivalent in their line of endeavour). It is far easier to pose as 'superior' to those who do have a go and it is much easier to criticise others from the safety of having no output to be compared to theirs.

The fact is that the majority of people do not have the will to do much about their dreams, because they give up before they begin. They are chronically apathetic.

This behaviour separates the influenced from the influencer!

THE BEST STRIKER WE NEVER HAD

A professional footballer, John, nearing the end of his

playing career at the age of 33, was having a (soft) drink with some pals. He was approached by Sandy, an old school mate, who somewhat belligerently told him that he, Sandy, had been much the better footballer when they played together as teenagers and that if he had stuck at the game, he would have been far more successful as a professional at senior level than John had been.

John agreed that this was 'probably true' but he pointed out to Sandy – who looked overweight, unfit and slightly drunk – that while he, slimmer and fitter, had stuck it out as a professional footballer, Sandy hadn't and what might have been 'never was and never would be'. The record books showed John's name not Sandy's, whose preferred lifestyle precluded the flowering of his football talents. Whatever skills John had shown in his teens, he could not abide the personal discipline needed to wear a professional club's shirt.

Every two years, a new crop of men and women go to Washington, DC to serve as Members of Congress in their first term on the bottom rung of the national political ladder of the United States.

Among one such crop, a young Congressman from Texas behaved strangely on the first morning of his term in a fairly ordinary budget hostel, not far from Capitol Hill. He was among several dozen other Congressional 'new boys' in the hostel, which was a good place from which to become familiar with the city before finding permanent accommodation of their own (though for 'permanent' read 'one term only', because some wouldn't win another election).

This young Congressman was up that first morning at 5.45 a.m. and he went straight to the communal showers. Once there, he stripped to a towel round his waist and commenced to wash and shave, slowly.

He introduced himself to every single other resident (like him, all new members of Congress) as they came in for a shower, carefully noting their names and the districts from which they came.

Next he took his shower and, instead of going back to his room, he returned to a sink to 'wash and shave' again – slowly. He dawdled and met the late arrivals – introducing himself as before. He took another shower – and another – and 'washed and shaved' again and again, slowly.

He quit his strange behaviour only after meeting every single new Congressman. He knew their names and was sure they would remember him for his big, friendly Texas welcome. They would also associate him with their first day in Congress.

The effort involved in getting up and hanging round the bathroom already separated him from all the others in that year's crop, and he showed throughout his career the same dedication to detail in everything else he did with and for people whom he wanted to influence, which probably explains why he served many more terms.

He also went on to become the senior Senator for Texas. Later he became Senate Majority Leader (the most influential politician in Washington, next to the President). Following the assassination of President Kennedy, he was sworn in as President. His name was Lyndon B. Johnson.

So what is it about the influencer that stands out?

It is the energy they deploy in pursuit of their goals. They don't just talk about what they might do, or what they could have done, or what might have been. Putting it bluntly, they get up in the morning. They subscribe to the GOYA principle, not in appreciation of Goya's art (though that is not entirely precluded), but in GOYA the acronym: 'Get Off Your Ass!'

And that is what influencers do. They go out and find time to meet the people they need to influence. They energise. They don't wait for events to influence them; they go out and influence the people who create events.

This cannot be done from an armchair – or a bar stool. It can only be done by physically going from place to place and seeing the people you must deal with face to face.

Also, they supplement (though do not safely substitute) much of their GOYA activity by GOTT: 'Get On The Telephone'.

Influencers use the telephone like it was free (that it isn't free is one of the costs of influence). Even here, where you would think that the lethargic would come into their own, they don't. Making calls requires less energy than criss-crossing town to see somebody, but the lethargic mostly don't even know the numbers to dial.

They stare blankly when asked if they have called Fred to tell him about Mary's memo. Variously, they thought somebody else would call Fred; that Fred was not available; that Mary's memo didn't have a chance anyway; that they were too busy; that they felt awkward; they weren't sure of Fred's views; and, in final demonstration of naïvety, that their call would not make any difference. This serial neglect of their interests causes deepening fatalism (in extreme cases, paranoia): the feeling that the world is 'against me'.

It is true that efforts at influencing on an *ad hoc*, occasional and intermittent basis are unlikely to succeed. Ringing Fred out of the blue to discuss something of more concern to you than Fred (and of whose relationship with Mary you are ignorant) is going to be ineffective and possibly counterproductive.

Your neglect of Fred before you need his support has a price — if he knows nothing of your interest in Mary's memo he will act without considering them; if you know nothing about his interest in Mary's memo you cannot help him. Either way, you are at the mercy of events (and that most uncomfortable of experiences, 'where ignorant armies clash by night').

So, an influencing strategy is not best cobbled together on a fire-fighting basis. You have to invest in influence, and the price of your investment is not money. The price is your effort, your time, your energy, your persistence and, above all, what you can do and have done to and for Fred (and all the other 'Freds', including Mary!).

IT DON'T TAKE MUCH TO KEEP IN TOUCH

Jake, a friend of mine, is a professional footballers' agent who represents players from all over the world, for whom he 'handles' contracts with clubs, their deals with sponsors, problems with anybody with whom they have 'problems' and, on top of this, he manages their careers.

As Jake puts it: 'Career management is more important than deal management', which notion comes from his years representing rock stars.

As well as this long-term outlook (unusual among his competitors) Jake has very precise ideas about attention to short-term details.

For one thing he regularly attends matches where one or more of his players are involved – this sometimes means visiting grounds well off the beaten track where his younger players are making their way through the junior leagues.

For another, he uses his mobile phone to maximum effect. He is seldom out of touch with any of his players on a regular basis for more than three days: he rings even if only to say 'Hello' and 'What's going on?' Naturally, he is available 24 hours a day for any of his players and his mobile is always on, even when he is abroad. Recently while we were watching a cup tie in Scotland, Jake was on his mobile talking to his local contact in Namibia.

Jake keeps in touch with other agents and football managers. He doesn't idly chat. He makes courtesy calls that last no more than a minute and only stays on if they lead the conversation into business.

As Jake says, 'it don't take much keep in touch.'

Your road to influence begins with getting off your ass and going – now, not next week – to see the people who can influence the outcome you seek. If you can't get to them face to face, then get on the telephone or the Internet, regularly and not just when you want something. This will cost you time and effort but nothing worthwhile having ever comes easily.

Sure, it might cost you the effort to cross a room to introduce yourself – Big Deal! – but I bet from time to time you have crossed a room for tasty snacks and a liquid refreshment or two for yourself. Why not do something, instead, for the guy across the room who may welcome some social attention? He might one day be in a position to influence a decision in your favour and your gesture could be the beginning of an influential relationship.

Senator Johnson was the supreme influencer: he learned early on that when you want to be more than just clean and close shaven, three showers are better than one.

ANSWERS TO SELF-ASSESSMENT TEST 2

1. (a)   No.
   (b)   No.
   (c)   No, no.
   (d)   Yes. You start with how the committee stands and then decide to what extent this indicates you should support/oppose the applications.

2. (a)   No, it may be too late to react effectively during the meeting.
   (b)   Better than (a) but not as good as (c)
   (c)   Yes, GOYA.

3. (a)   Yes, you will need to take the initiative in the situations. Meet new people.
   (b)   Not as good as (a) but can follow (a) – they may be desperate to talk to someone they know and are too timid to try (a).
   (c)   No, not in the influence game.

SELF-ASSESSMENT TEST 3

1. You are in a fairly routine job that does not stretch you. You do not appear to be making any progress in your quest to raise your profile in the firm. Do you:
   (a) complain at every opportunity of your boredom and dissatisfaction?
   (b) look for opportunities to take on more responsibilities, even in routine tasks?
   (c) only undertake (b) if the tasks are commensurate with your status?

2. Clearly your rapid rise in an organisation is due to the sponsorship of a single powerful personage. Do you:
   (a) keep close to the personage and distance yourself from his rivals?
   (b) distance yourself from the personage and keep close to his rivals?
   (c) keep close to the personage and his rivals?

3. Most people in your organisation play golf and socialise as a company group. You know nothing about golf and think it a waste of time. Do you:
   (a) take up golf?
   (b) refuse to take up golf?
   (c) find some way to become associated with the social activities focused on golf?

CHAPTER 3

The fickle finger of fate

or how to benefit from a backwater

Napoleon favoured 'lucky Generals' (it's not recorded what his lucky Generals favoured). Talent is all very well, but luck cannot be beaten as the final ingredient of success.

History is replete with people whose talents were compromised by events. I know of one talented man well known to cinema fans for all the wrong reasons who was treated cruelly by fate. He gained the sponsorship of men of influence but events robbed him of the prizes to which, by all accounts, he yearned.

As a young man he was picked out of obscurity by the great navigator, then at the height of his fame, Captain James Cook, and was assured of his future by Cook's warm regard for the cartographic, navigational and seamanship talents that he displayed during Cook's fateful Third Voyage to the Pacific. Unfortunately, Cook was killed by Hawaiians during that voyage. His officers, jealous of the young seaman, made sure that Cook's young protégé went back to obscurity.

Later, he became the protégé of another prominent man of his day, Sir Joseph Banks, who wangled it with King George III to send him on another voyage to the Pacific. That voyage too, ended in a career disaster because he took with him as one of his juniors, a moody malcontent called Fletcher Christian, whose mother's bankruptcy had forced him from a gentleman scholar's career into the rough life of the Royal Navy. I speak, of course, of William Bligh, of HMS *Bounty*, a man who must surely have lamented: 'if only . . . '.

There are many who have been treated with great generosity by fate. And there are as many others who missed their chances because they did not recognise what fate had dealt them.

So, recognising the luck of opportunity is a characteristic of the would-be influencer. It's no good being a lucky General without a war in which to demonstrate your talent. It's no good being in the right place at the right time, if you don't take advantage of fate's blessings. Nor is it much good recognising opportunity if you have insufficient talents to exploit what fate delivers.

But, if you are talented and unrecognised, exploiting an opportunity to influence those who can give you a big hand upwards is the next best thing to writing your own pay cheque.

Take, William ('Bill') Coleman who had joined the Bank at the same time as several other ambitious young people, all of whom had risen with him from branch tellers to the lower reaches of management and all of whom had since left him well behind while his career stalled.

Bill was disappointed about what happened and his disappointments deepened by watching the subsequent progress of newer recruits who also overtook him in the promotion stakes. When he met with his contemporaries at Bank functions he avoided conversation on matters of substance and was embarrassed when the friendly banter from the past petered out.

'I was thinking of quitting the Bank,' Bill told me one evening some years later when he was explaining how he had subsequently risen to the most senior position of all the men and women who had joined the Bank with him. 'This almost came to a head when I was transferred from Head Office in London to the Rutford Branch. Madge was pregnant again and we couldn't really afford to move house.'

Bill was given a routine clerical job checking paperwork supporting loan applications in a tiny office at the back of the building, overlooking the dustbins. To career depression was added the boredom of doing work well below his abilities. He mused whether this was the Bank's way of subtly hinting he should seek another career elsewhere.

A few days into his job, with several drafts of a resignation letter crumpled in the bin, the phone rang. It was the Bank's Area Manager from Leeds. 'Have you anything left for Saturday?' asked the caller. Bill didn't know what she was talking about.

'Sorry?' started Bill, but was interrupted before he could explain that she must have the wrong extension.

'Look, it's my major customer who is threatening to quit over some standing order cock-ups, so you must do something. He's a fanatical United supporter and I need four tickets for Saturday's match to keep him sweet. Do what you can and call me back – I'll be in the Bradford branch from 11.'

EXILED TO DESTINY

In Turkey's turbulent years near the end of the Ottoman Empire, a secular dissident in the armed forces was exiled to the far north of Asian Turkey. The government wanted to remove his influence on the political events that were rocking the old regime in Ankara and the place they chose for his exile was close to a place called the Dardanelles.

The *ancien régime's* plans worked well for a while because the Dardanelles were a long way from the capital. But fate dealt the exiled officer a winning hand. Unbeknown to his tormentors, the British chose to invade Turkey – at the Dardanelles.

The British plans were fairly sound, as far as amphibious landings using longboats were concerned, but the invasion soon ran into trouble from unexpected and obstinate resistance from local Turkish forces. As the British, Australian, New Zealand and Indian troops went ashore, the exiled officer arrived and took command of the sparse Turkish forces stationed in the area and organised a brilliant defence (aided by monumental incompetence between the Royal Navy and the Army command).

The national prestige gained by the defeat of the British forces at the Dardanelles was instrumental in the exiled officer's rise to power. If he had failed as a soldier he would have failed as a political force.

If the Ottomans had sent Kemal Attaturk into exile on the Iraqi border he probably would have vanished into the obscurity they intended for him. Instead, they exiled him to the north – and the rest, as they say, is history.

Bill was puzzled but forgot about the call in minutes. Twenty minutes later another call came through, this time from Moira, somebody he knew in the first branch he had worked in when he joined the Bank. She asked how he was doing and they exchanged pleasantries. Then she turned to business.

'Mark asked me to call when he noticed your transfer to your new position in the Staff News – congratulations by the way – and told me to tell you that he would regard it as a great favour if you could get him two tickets for the United match.'

'Look, Moira,' said the by now perplexed Bill, 'what makes you think I can get tickets just because I'm in Rutford? This is a Bank, remember.'

'I know it is not easy this late to get two tickets,' she said, ignoring Bill's question, 'but you surely can do something for an old friend? Mark hopes you might be able to something.'

'Why?'

'Because, one of your new responsibilities, Bill, is the Bank's box at United. Have they not explained that to you yet?'

'Er, no, not quite. They've been too busy I suppose. Tell me, what am I supposed to do?'

'I don't know, but Mark said that with you at Rutford, it was his lucky day.'

Bill promised he would do what he could. Immediately he put

the phone down he searched through the drawers of his desk and the filing cabinets. One cabinet was locked, until he found the keys in the desk.

It took him an hour to read through all the documents and the correspondence he found. They confirmed what Moira had said. Apparently he was in charge of the Bank's private box at United. It sat 12 people per match for lunch and the match, plus another 12, who joined the Bank's lunch table but sat in the open stand.

There were details of every match for the rest of the season and some sheets showed many branches had already booked places, but there were as many blank spaces, including six for Saturday's United–Leeds match. Bill sat back and thought about this turn in events. No wonder there was not enough Bank business to keep him busy in his new post! The hospitality work, he realised, would keep him busy.

As if on cue, the phone rang again, this time for tickets from the Nottingham branch. Then the Area Manager for East Anglia rang, seeking tickets for later in the month.

It didn't take long for Bill to see that instead of a clerical backwater, he was sitting on a career gold-mine. He had been given discretion over corporate hospitality at a major football club, with potential demand for his services from across the entire Bank's network.

It wasn't that the Bank was full of United supporters (Bill certainly wasn't, as he preferred Rugby League). Nor did they have to be that keen on football, because it was a social package followed by chances to meet the players and the club's famous manager and to get autographs for the children.

If enough people in the Bank wanted tickets, Bill realised his career could turn towards the sunlight. And that is what it did, he told me.

He started with the Area Manager in Leeds and then worked his way round the Bank's upper echelons to get himself known, sometimes responding to requests and sometimes initiating shrewd suggestions to certain people when something for their area was on offer.

He piled up favours and made sure that he demonstrated his social skills at every opportunity, by attending the matches to superintend the details and to liaise with United's hospitality staff. This also put him in touch with senior staff at many business corporations who were the Bank's customers, and with many others who were important customers of other banks.

He got to know the high-profile football players and could always arrange for them to do promotions for Bank customers. There was also a steady demand from Bank staff and customers for autographs, scarves and football memorabilia, all of which he arranged willingly.

He served at Rutford for six years, moving several grades up the managerial hierarchy and leaping over all of his former rivals. From Rutford he moved into Marketing and then on to what he is today, Director of Public Affairs, where one of his first acts was to move the hospitality desk into his own department (where he is keeping a weather eye on Heather, whom he promoted to see what she would do with her opportunity).

ACTIVITY 7

What backwater are you in? Are you sure it is a backwater?

Now, I am not suggesting that a career-ticket is hidden in a locked cabinet in the corner of your office space, though its equivalent could very well be staring you in the face.

The first steps from an opportunity to a success will only be taken if you look for them. Having found them, your next task is to plan how you will use the opportunity to extend your influence.

You still have much work to do, but you know that, don't you?

ANSWERS TO SELF-ASSESSMENT TEST 3

1. (a) No. You undermine your reputation by embarrassing those who could help you.

(b) Look for opportunities to take on more responsibilities, even in routine tasks? Yes. Do something about it and make yourself indispensable.

(c) Absolutely not. If you had real status you would not be in this predicament.

2. (a) A sure invitation for fate to exploit your vulnerability. If anything happens to your sponsor – death in service, transfer to another organisation, loss of office with the organisation, and suchlike – his rivals will retaliate once he can no longer protect you.

(b) Only if you are a kamikaze pilot.

(c) Yes. Be nice to people on your way up – you might need them when you meet them on your way down.

3. (a) Maybe, if you find you have an aptitude for it.

(b) Not a good idea to cut yourself off in this manner.

(c) Yes, if (a) does not work out, can you run the golf outings, act as factotum for the golf socials, do the donkey work as an organiser?

SELF-ASSESSMENT TEST 4

1. You are a shift supervisor in a manufacturing plant and want to move up the management ladder. Your section is fully stretched meeting its targets because of a recent reduction in the head-count. The fork lift drivers who work directly with your production teams are under your hourly instruction. For all other matters – pay, holidays, hours of work, grievance, discipline, etc., – they are managed by the Transport Department, to whom they nominally report, though, in practice, they have very little to do with these people. Do you:
   (a) leave the situation alone because it is historical rather than functional?
   (b) recommend that the shift fork lift drivers be transferred to your control?
   (c) ask the drivers which department they would rather work for?

2. Your boss suggests that you might be interested in taking on the running of a new project in addition to your current responsibilities. This would mean considerable extra work for you: Do you:
   (a) say 'yes', if you are promoted and your pay increased?
   (b) ask when the new responsibilities will be reflected in your pay?
   (c) say 'yes'?

3. You hear of a new development in the means by which your department's products could be delivered. The new development, if successful, will widen the market for your company's output. Personnel in other departments are

27

just as capable as you of initiating the new developments. Do you:

(a) volunteer your services as a project leader from the beginning?
(b) hold back while you check out the impact of the new development on your current work roles?
(c) suggest somebody in one of the other departments who would do a good job as a project leader?

CHAPTER 4:

'HELP!' is not just a four-letter word

or how to help yourself to a better future

Some lonely people, who consider themselves tough (the two states of mind often go together), would never admit to asking anyone for help. During their late night litanies of advice for tough guys, they readily advise themselves never to seek help, never to offer it and never to respond to requests for it. Help is just not in their vocabulary or within their understanding.

For an influencer, help is much more than a four-letter word. It is a powerful currency for creating, exchanging and exercising influence. It is both a strategic objective and a tactical instrument.

Whatever else the ladder to success is composed of there are certain to be large dollops of people helping each other up it. It is almost conceivable that influence can be exercised by somebody who does not seek, nor dispense, help from or to those who have the capacity to offer it or a desire to receive it. But this would be a very exceptional case and, like most exceptional cases, it would not be a good idea to make your career dependent on it.

ACTIVITY 8

Whom have you asked for help recently? Who has asked you to help them?

People like to help as much as they like to be helped. Mostly, they only have to be asked. The fact that many ambitious people don't like to ask for help (of a direct kind) leaves a lot of scope for those other people who overcome these inhibitions and do ask others for help.

BECAUSE I WAS ASKED

An ex-Congressman surprised a number of his party colleagues when he publicly supported the campaign of an 'unknown no-hoper', who had brazenly declared himself to be a US Presidential candidate and had joined a crowded field of more famous hopefuls.

His friends chided him for supporting a 'nobody' against the powerful and well-known national candidates who could do more for him when in his own re-election campaign.

When pressed on why he had decided to throw his lot in with the unknown, he replied: 'He is the only candidate who knocked on my front door and asked me to help in his campaign, hence I said "yes".'

A year later, the unknown nobody won the Democratic Party nomination and went on to become President of the United States. His name was Jimmy Carter.

And the ex-Congressman went on to become a Senator with the new President's endorsement.

The well-known national figures who didn't ask for his help became less well-known, but it is unlikely that they learned the lesson: ask if you want to receive.

Conventional wisdom opines that it is easier to ask for help from colleagues of roughly equal status in the organisation than to ask a boss to help you. The received wisdom appeals to intuitive reasoning. Bosses may react negatively to a request for help. And if you make too many requests for help they might conclude that you lack initiative and can't do your job.

Colleagues are not just people of equal status. They are also potential rivals and asking them for help not only implies some dependence on them, it also creates an obligation. Bringing someone into a project reveals to them possible opportunities for their own advancement and this may induce them to make a 'takeover bid' for your initiative or, at the very least, stimulate them to press for a large share of the glory.

This probably explains why many requests for help are directed towards lower-status people in your organisation, or people who are quite clearly junior partners in your initiatives. Some junior people are happy to play this role because they see it as an opportunity for them. You should never forget that you are not the only person in the organisation who seeks more influence – that smiling, bright-eyed and energetic junior may be putting her first foot on your ladder to rise with – or over – you! Flying on the coat-tails of a fast rising star may be just the lift she needs.

ACTIVITY 9

On whose coat-tails did you ride to where you are today, and on whose might you ride to where you want to be?

The search for help begins, quite properly, with the sensible caution of testing out your ideas for changes or initiatives with selected people around you before you float them into the organisation firmly attached to your name. This is basic to the cultivation of your influence. But be cautious.

You will have many ideas and solutions (some of which are plain silly or otherwise impractical) leaving a few that qualify to be taken seriously by others. The best way to filter your flow of ideas into runners and (embarrassing) non-runners, is to float them past allies rather than random 'friends'.

Always remember that in practice ideas and solutions to organisational problems are not judged solely on their merits. Just because your 'friends' like the idea, it does not follow it 'has legs'. They may be poor judges. They may encourage you because they like you. They may be in no position to appreciate the significance of what you propose.

The fun begins when you go public. For a start, some people react to other people's ideas because they were 'not invented here'. They are against your ideas because they did not think of them first. Moreover, if they are jealous of you, their inventor, they are doubly opposed to your ideas on emotional grounds. Their hostility may be based on the fear that you, the originator, will reap 'undeserved' credit or some other benefit, like the friendly notice of the bosses.

It makes sense, therefore, to try out your solutions to problems with trustworthy colleagues first, rather than casual friendly faces. If trustworthy colleagues, whom you respect for their seriousness, respond positively – even offer supportive suggestions – enrol them into your alliance to affect the change.

Ask them for advice on whom else should you consult? They might make some useful suggestions. They might also sponsor introductions to other players who can influence the outcome. Ideas that survive this filtering process, however, remain fragile.

Do not just line up support and leave them with no further role. If the change is radical, it takes effort to iron out all the defects and, because you cannot see or anticipate every contingency, all plans begin but need not end with inbuilt defects.

Allies provide useful feedback on the workability of what you propose. If your allies can spot defects and flaws, your rivals will surely do likewise which they will exploit to discredit you and your proposals.

Tap into your support by keeping allies informed of any contemplated changes to make the plan workable, and carefully consider their comments, criticisms and suggestions. They are not the enemy (until you learn otherwise to the contrary). Your plan has to become their plan too if your influencing project is to make progress.

The 'help' phase of any influencing project is always threatened by a 'takeover' by other players, who see your initiative as more beneficial to them if they, rather than you, sponsor it. This could be a critical moment. Some attempted takeovers are benign and necessary to implement the change; others are malign, such as when rivals take over the change project to deny you the credit.

At this point you must decide on your motives for proposing the change. Are you out solely to enhance your own credibility and prospects, or is the proposed change a genuine solution to a real problem in the organisation? These need not be mutually exclusive.

Which of these motives for you is uppermost? They are both legitimate, but if the enhancement of your own position is more important for you than solving the organisation's problem, you are more likely to resent a takeover. If, however, the organisation's problem is uppermost, you are more likely to welcome takeovers if it assists the adoption of the change.

Your welcome must remain cautious – you suspect them of opportunism, perhaps – but if their commitment to the change is helpful and necessary, you may have to share credit with them and, perhaps, forgo it altogether. But all is not lost if this happens.

The litmus test is whether their intervention is necessary to implement the change. If it is, the organisation benefits. Your allies know who initiated the change and credit you accordingly. When what you initiate is seen to be implemented by senior management, your credibility is enhanced. When powerful people respond positively to your influencing projects, you acquire credibility by association.

ACTIVITY 10

Have you suffered a 'takeover' of something you initiated and for which subsequently you received little or no credit? How do you feel about that?

The alternative of monopolising ownership of all your initiatives and, in fits of pique, repelling pirates who attempt to take them over, significantly damages your credibility. While building your influence in an organisation, it is better not to be disparaged as too possessive to be a team player. Anybody powerful enough to take over your solutions will have no qualms in squashing your attempt to hang on to them – and likely will discredit you while so doing.

What about rivals on the same level as yourself who attempt 'takeovers' of your initiatives? The best response is to welcome their involvement and then 'out-GOYA' them. You are the link between the disparate allies who support the change and you therefore energise the process between inception and delivery. Tactically, you must delegate and closely monitor the outputs of individuals who undertake to complete tasks in aid of the project.

Set them 'SMART' objectives when delegating. All delegated tasks must be:

Specific
Measurable
Achievable
Realistic
Time bound.

If you delegate SMART tasks to people who you suspect are trying to 'take over' your project for their own ends, their achievement of the SMART objectives (provided these individuals meet them!) will benefit your initiative. You also sort out the wheat from the chaff when some of these individuals fail to deliver what they agreed to do.

Using SMART criteria tests the motives of those who try to take over your project. If they successfully deliver, this helps you; if they fail, their attempted usurpation is easily rebuffed and their credibility is easily damaged.

But beware of paranoia.

Most of your early influencing projects are unlikely to be major transformations in an organisation. They are more likely to be relatively minor projects, which opportunistic rivals are unlikely to usurp. When the stakes are much higher, there may be serious threats to the project's paternity but by then you will be a formidable player, not a beginner. Also, by then your allies will have formed a reliable coalition with you, which is not easy for hostile rivals to take over because they are used to working with rather than against you.

ANSWERS TO SELF-ASSESSMENT TEST 4

1. (a) No – unless you discover good reasons why you should leave the situation alone. While it is separate, you are vulnerable if the drivers become upset by aspects of their pay and conditions beyond your control.
   (b) Yes – if you construct a good case for so doing.
   (c) Might be a good idea to check this out before you try to move them. A sudden refusal to move on their part after you go public would reveal a flaw in your judgement.

2. (a) Difficult to carry through in practice (I know because this is a subject of many e-letters sent to my HELPLINE). Sounds somewhat threatening, I am told.
   (b) Yes. Sets a clear intention on your part without threatening as in (a).
   (c) Could be appropriate if it is an opportunity to show what you can do but not as assertive as (b). Depends on your firm's culture.

3. (a) Bold move for a seriously ambitious person.
   (b) Cautious move if you are unsure of yourself. While checking, somebody else could step in.
   (c) You are not a seriously ambitious person.

SELF-ASSESSMENT TEST 5

1. A colleague at the weekly management meeting offers to collect items for the staffing report due at the end of the week, presents an analysis of the print overruns she has collected from past reports and passes round pre-prepared offprints of some of the boss's articles from the trade press. Do you conclude:
   (a) she is 'brown nosing' as nobody asked her to do any of this?
   (b) she is volunteering for some purpose not yet apparent?
   (c) you are overly suspicious?

2. A colleague advises you, 'never volunteer for anything' because it is a 'mug's game to let them exploit you'. Is this:
   (a) advice from a wise, if slightly cynical, friend?
   (b) advice from a foolish and more than slightly cynical friend?
   (c) advice from a devious rival?

3. Your boss asks you to take on some project work normally conducted by people a grade above you. She mentions nothing about promotion up a grade, or about extra money for the heavier responsibilities. You find in your pay that month an increase but your pleasure subsides when your colleagues also report the same pay rise and none of them have taken on extra work. Do you:
   (a) complain to your colleagues about the unfairness of the boss?
   (b) ask the boss about your prospects for promotion and a rise?
   (c) refuse the extra responsibilities without extra pay and promotion?

(d) continue with your new responsibilities and raise these questions several months later when you have proven your capabilities?

CHAPTER 5

Who's afraid of extra work?

or how to be 'volunteered'

When your boss wants you to do something, he or she relies on something called 'charisma', 'leadership' or 'motivation'. Considerable training effort is put into showing managers how to inspire their subordinates using 'top-down' management styles, making 'leadership' the most funded research topic in management schools.

So, managing downwards, well or badly, is pretty well understood and widely practised by bosses who have the responsibility, the authority, the power and a plethora of rewards and punishments to enact their top down controls.

Influencing, by way of contrast, is about managing upwards and sideways and is not so well understood, nor so widely practised. With 'downsizing', the flattening of organisational structures and the preference for consensual management styles, influencing is spreading in and across organisations.

ACTIVITY 11

What do you do when you need to persuade the boss to do something he or she would not normally do, or hasn't thought of doing, but which you value?

Upwards influencing is usually accompanied by the absence of authority and power. Unlike a boss, you usually do not have any rewards to offer those who help you to achieve your objectives. You have to secure your ends with new techniques and tools, perhaps inventing and improvising as you go along.

Starting from where you are in the organisation, you seek certain outcomes and, to be successful, you need influencing techniques that work. Where you learn to influence can be a lottery within your organisation.

As you move from one organisation to another, you learn to recognise how your colleagues jostle to extend their influence. If you have a modicum of political awareness, you also learn to recognise when someone is trying to influence you, or to recognise that a rival is attempting to influence your colleagues or your boss, and when it is appropriate to intervene to assist or obstruct somebody else's influencing activity.

ACTIVITY 12

When were you last aware that somebody's behaviour suggested they were up to something in the organisation? Can you recollect exactly what they were doing and what led you to conclude they were trying to influence somebody else?

Awareness gives you an edge over less aware colleagues and inept or inexperienced players. It includes identifying the goals of their influencing activities. Otherwise, their influencing remains a jumble of 'smart' moves without a goal. Players who play politics for the sake of it have low esteem, are not taken seriously and are often treated as a menace (because they are a menace!) in most organisations.

It's not enough to know the moves that facilitate influence. You have to know how to read the game as well, if you wish to excel in what you do.

A defender who charges up the field in pursuit of the ball and has difficulty getting back to defend the gap he left behind would be severely chastised by his manager if his conduct cost his team the game. A batsman raising the run rate and the risk of being bowled out, when told to play for time and fewer runs, would not be considered a useful team player. So consider your objectives before you influence. It might save you running round like a headless chicken – and a player with no influence.

One object of influencing is to have new tasks and responsibilities assigned to you or your unit. Sounds simple enough and is, but it is not always easy to implement: too cack-handed in your attempt to extend your responsibilities and you are vulnerable to charges of empire building.

For almost every influencing tactic you are likely to use, there is an associated comment that belittles your efforts. Rivals do not restrain themselves from disparaging remarks when it is in their interest to block your efforts. So charges like empire building are probably the mildest of the rebukes you will receive.

ACTIVITY 13

What are the common put-downs used in your line of work?

Why then should you seek out new responsibilities? At the very least, to prevent them being taken over by others. Extending the area over which you exercise responsibility stakes your claim to advancement (the cognoscenti call it the 'gold field principle'). If you don't acquire new responsibilities, your rivals will, and if this loss of opportunity continues long enough you could be left well behind in the race up the Yukon!

By definition, the person with the biggest responsibility – assuming you exhibit competence in everything you are responsible for – is the person with the largest influence in the organisation.

The top boss, who is responsible for everything the organisation does, has the greatest influence by virtue of position; your influence grows to the extent that, and at the rate at which, your responsibilities grow and are seen to grow.

Consider Andrew, one of several bright young MBAs, working as a manager in Omega, a computer software firm in Europe. He worked alongside a team of 'rocket scientists', all technically brilliant and totally absorbed in preparing an upgrade to Image-Maker®, one of Omega's bestselling software tools for the PC market.

Andrew's job was to ensure that the upgrade was kept in front of the opinion-makers in the PC market, that it was publicised in the specialist magazines and web sites, and that current customers knew about the functionality of forthcoming upgrades, so that they would wait for them in preference to switching to rival products.

His job kept Andrew quite busy and involved much international travel, including to head office in Seattle. Mainly, it was fairly routine once he had done the rounds of everybody important in the field and had attended the main software exhibitions and conferences.

Omega software was sold through retailers in just about every country in the world and ImageMaker® had enjoyed a high market penetration until recently, following the shipping of VisionMaker®, a new rival product from Bothwell Software Systems Ltd in Lanark.

During a recent visit to Taiwan to visit a major PC assembler company, Andrew, in casual conversation over dinner, heard from their marketing people that they had been approached by a database software manufacturer to embed their programs into their PCs as they were manufactured. The database firm was willing to provide its programs at an extremely attractive price (less than a tenth of the retail price available from the usual dealers). The Taiwanese PC manufacturer was 'thinking this over', Andrew was told.

On the long flight home Andrew thought about this revolutionary development (which today is now common practice; at the time it was unheard of) and what it would mean for software distribution. If PCs were sold with software already installed, how would retail dealers make their money and how would software designers recover their development costs? Above all, how would this development affect ImageMaker® profits?

Back in Scotland, Andrew reported to his boss on his trip to

Taiwan and he raised as a new marketing strategy the prior installation of ImageMaker® at the PC manufacturing stage. His boss seemed interested though not excited, so Andrew suggested that he be put in charge of assessing the marketing possibilities, including the viability of recovering development costs and making profits. He undertook to explore the idea with several branded PC manufacturers and distributors. He also needed to gauge the reaction of head office in Seattle, which he was to visit the following week, and volunteered to report back within three weeks. If his report was positive, he suggested, his boss could send a proposal to the board. His boss agreed and Andrew got on with the new task, in addition to his normal duties.

Now in IT, such volunteering may be regular enough to be almost routine and people in the business hardly think it unusual to seek new responsibilities or to promote new initiatives (something to do with the average age being under 25?). Still, Andrew's experience illustrates the applicability of this influencing objective to any organisation or business sector more staid than IT.

Taking over new tasks or initiatives in a culture that thrives on innovation is one thing; taking over existing tasks undertaken by other departments, in cultures where the employees exercise protective claims over them, is much more difficult and should only be attempted when you prepare the ground well, otherwise you might start a 'turf war' and lose it.

Individuals as well as work units can extend their influence by having new responsibilities assigned to them, either by passive acquiescence or by formal and contested acknowledgement from the boss.

BETTER TO BE WISE THAN NOT WANTED

Marie, a project manager with an economics consultancy, was ambitious, energetic and relatively poorly paid. She was approached by her boss who wanted her to take over a major research project on behalf of a potential inward investor.

The work was within her capability and entailed senior-level meetings with the client, the application of advanced statistical computer analysis, and the writing of reports that would give her high-level exposure in her own and the client organisation.

She asked her boss for a pay rise and to be promoted up a grade. As she was on a short-term contract with one year to run and the project would take two years, she also wanted an extension formalised in her employment contract, or a transfer to the firm's permanent staff. Her boss said none of these would be possible at this moment but he would look at her requests again within six months.

She asked her friend what to do. He advised her to take on the job and to make herself so indispensable that her boss would have no choice but to extend her contract and raise her pay when he could see visible results from her work.

Marie declined this advice and stuck out for her demands. Her boss eventually withdrew the job offer, claiming his hands were tied, reassigned Marie to a short-term project and did not extend her contract.

Later, Marie took the firm to an employment tribunal claiming unfair dismissal. Her friend thought privately that it was a pity that there was no tribunal for 'unwise decisions'.

Many a lowly employee has extended her ambit of control in her job by assuming new responsibilities and, by making herself relatively indispensable, successfully pushing a claim for promotion (when your bosses initiate such programmes they call it 'job enrichment', which, ironically, some employees resist).

ACTIVITY 14

Look around your job arena and list some possible opportunities to extend your responsibilities.

Career-minded people are advised to lay the foundations for their advancement by looking for opportunities to widen their responsibilities well beyond the confines of whatever grade they are in.

Understanding the detailed working of the organisation's procedures, or coping with the idiosyncrasies of filing and cataloguing systems, or the functionality of computer networks and programs, separates you from your unversed colleagues and gives you that first step up the ladder. Your expertise must be demonstrated to your seniors and you must exploit all opportunities to do so on a regular basis. Extending your expertise in such matters also supports your influencing objectives. Conversely, ignoring or, worse, deliberately avoiding or actively resisting opportunities to do so is certain to undermine your influence.

Justin, a colleague of mine many years ago, often described how he went out of his way at this or that meeting not to take on any responsibilities other than the ones he had already, though he was given many openings by his boss to assert his claims to new projects.

There is, of course, no obligation on anybody to seek out extra work roles and Justin made it clear where he stood on this subject on more than one occasion. He also told me, however, how angry he felt at suffering repeated 'promotion bypasses' with the same fervour that he boasted of his manoeuvres to avoid extra work. He claimed that his boss was 'prejudiced' against him, which was probably true after her experience of his attitudes over several years.

Getting extra work assigned to you is the key to influencing upwards. Compulsory assignment of work downwards to subordinates is a normal function of management. Bear it in mind that your boss is probably more used to dealing with 'pressed men' rather than volunteers.

ACTIVITY 15

Do you know anybody like Justin? If he sounds a bit like yourself you must consider seriously the damage you may be doing to your influence.

Justin's career never got off the ground, while Andrew's took off when he acted on some casual remarks at a boozy dinner in downtown Taipei. The difference between them is that one of them saw and took the opportunity that the other allowed to pass him by.

ANSWERS TO SELF-ASSESSMENT TEST 5

1. (a) Maybe she is a workaholic and maybe she can't help volunteering. More likely she has a reason.
   (b) Yes, your safest conclusion. Now investigate why.
   (c) Maybe. But not until you have tried (b).

2. (a) Maybe a friend who is slightly cynical but not somebody who is wise.
   (b) Maybe more than slightly cynical, even a friend, but someone who is certainly foolish.
   (c) More than likely.

3. (a) No. Always keep your own counsel. If you speak to anyone make sure he or she is a neutral and proven good friend (which is not the same as being 'friendly').
   (b) Not advisable if you are stressed by the situation. Better to try (d).
   (c) No. A foolish and short-sighted move. Organisations are littered with opinionated non-volunteers who seldom progress.
   (d) Yes.

SELF-ASSESSMENT TEST 6

1. You manage a purchasing function and discover that your staff spend 30 per cent of their time reconciling invoices with despatch notes from suppliers. You consider this to be an inefficient use of their time and you want them to spend less time on such clerical work. Do you:
   (a) instruct 'Goods Inward' to be more careful when checking their paperwork?
   (b) tell Purchasing staff to speed up the process of reconciling the paperwork?
   (c) ask one of your staff to find out the root causes of the problem and to initiate the necessary changes to resolve them?

2. You are a new manager in a major aircraft plant and observe that next to the main airframe assembly shed there is a large stores building containing, you are informed, all the aircraft parts that have been delivered by suppliers but not yet processed for release to assembly 'because there are discrepancies in their paperwork'. Assembly work is often interrupted because of a shortage of supplied components that await clearance in the stores building and which have been there, sometimes, for several weeks. Is this:
   (a) a defensible procedure to ensure the integrity of the airframe's components and the safe use of your aircraft?
   (b) a ludicrous example of bureaucracy gone mad, which only adds to costs and serves no really useful purpose, except to give power to paper shufflers?
   (c) Neither?

3. You want to make a concerted effort to demonstrate your managerial potential. Should you:

(a) look for an opportunity to undertake a small but not too challenging project to change the way your department works with another department?

(b) look for an opportunity to undertake a large and challenging project to change the way your department works with another department?

(c) wait until you are invited by the boss to undertake a project?

CHAPTER 6

Caroline's Way

or how to change behaviour

Getting people to change the way they behave, especially if it is the way 'we do things around here', is one the most difficult of influencing objectives. Accordingly, if you succeed it is a certain path upwards in your organisation.

Ordinarily, managers are well used to directing how jobs shall be done (and who by) and, if they want to change anything, they have a vast number of ways to achieve their objectives. It's typical of 'top-down management': the top tells those below what to do and when and how to do it.

Managing upwards is different. You have no authority over the way a boss or your colleagues work and none at all over people in other organisations. Yet there are many occasions in which how a job is done is as important to you as the fact that it is done. Changing behaviour at the best of times is never easy because the inbuilt resistance to change is universal.

ALL CHANGE!

Years ago, some trainees were acting as if they needed to be shaken up a bit, so lethargic had they become and appeared intent on remaining. They were declining into soporific indifference to learning. So I told everybody by name to change their seating places, directing some to cross the floor and others to swap seats with their immediate neighbours.

Now, my instructions were not difficult to comprehend or to implement, but the body language exhibited by most of the trainees in the three minutes (a long time, when there is palpable tension) needed to carry it out, was as intimidating as any I can remember. It was touch and go for a few seconds. I did not repeat the experiment physically, deciding it was better as a mind game to answer the question: 'How would you feel if I told you to change places?'

ACTIVITY 16

How touchy are you when it comes to someone telling you to change the way something is done?

Where the target of your influence, upon whom you depend for the success of your project, is superior to you or outside the ambit of your authority the normal resistance to change is intensified out of sight. They will resist and, because of the total absence of direct authority, they are easily provoked into resentment by attempts to tell them what to do. Even if you suggest that they consider doing something differently they soon make clear they won't.

Workplace cultures can be severely inefficient and nevertheless continue without challenge (other than feebly by those directly affected). People in key functions can behave in ways that undermine the commitment of the organisation to certain of its goals. For example, they might continue with forms of subtle discrimination prohibited by company policy or they might hold on to information which they have been encouraged to share with rivals in other functions. This is not an isolated phenomenon found occasionally in a few organisations. It is widespread in even the 'best in class' organisations, and it testifies to the triumph of irrational behaviour over common sense.

At a successful and profitable organisation of impeccable quality, I witnessed how they addressed a problem commonly found in many manufacturing plants: the 'battle' between production and stores. Allegedly, there is a characteristic of stores the world over to forget on whose side they are supposed to be working (I speak, of course, as someone from a production background!).

ACTIVITY 17

If you work in a manufacturing or processing business, how is the state of affairs between stores and the rest of the employees?

Those familiar with the layout of a traditional stores function will recognise the tiny hatch, often shut tight, through which they transact their business with the 'outside' world. Apart from the tiny hatch, when it is open, there is no other aperture through which anybody outside the stores can observe anybody, or anything, inside the stores. What goes on in the stores and what is stored there is a sacred mystery into which only stores personnel are inducted.

Production departments require regular access to stores for replacement parts, tools and consumables (all heavily 'guarded' by rigid procedures for access and retrieval) to complete each shift. The system in this particular company prevented production from accessing the stores, irrespective of the urgency of the requirement, without a great deal of difficulty and frustrating hassle. Though widely known at all levels of management and discussed regularly at meetings, nothing was done about it because of the widespread aversion to confronting layers of past behavioural 'atrocities'.

The problem defied occasional interventions of higher management to improve matters and, in consequence, it slipped to the bottom of their agenda. Appeals for more co-operation and reasonable relationships fell on deaf ears as production and stores blamed each other and allowed the gulf to deepen between them.

ACTIVITY 18

Are there any apparently 'intractable' disputes between departments in your place of work? Which side, if any, has your sympathy?

Into this quagmire stepped Caroline, a newly hired ambitious junior materials manager who was determined to make her mark. She soon became aware of the 'stores problem' from her regular visits to production and she soon learned about the 'production problem' from stores (she was well practised in GOYA). Being a newcomer, she had no axe to grind for either party. Indeed, she felt the whole business was a bit silly, but restrained herself from commenting that the grown-ups were acting like children. She realised that rational argument and appeals to common sense from her would be futile. The answer could only come from the people who were committed to fighting a senseless dispute.

Caroline did two things.

First, she noted that stores was indirectly a sub-unit of materials management, and so she asked her boss for leave to tackle the problem. Her boss agreed, he told me, without much enthusiasm or hope for her prospects, because all others had failed.

Second, Caroline volunteered to initiate in her role as a junior materials manager a series of 'Quality Group' meetings between production and stores, to which she sent an open invitation to managers to attend or to send a representative. She included with the invitation an agenda which included the item 'New Procedures'.

The first fortnightly meeting of the Quality Group was attended by fairly junior representatives, as was the second, perhaps reflecting senior managers' view of the importance of meetings called by a relatively junior employee. Caroline was undeterred, she told me, and I commented that persistence was a characteristic of people about to make their mark.

The early meetings didn't reach the 'New Procedures' item due to the prolonged, and often animated, discussions on other agenda items. She dropped hints to everybody attending about what she had in mind, supplemented by vague briefings when, on trips around the plant, she was asked about her plans (clearly, the word got round via the firm's proverbial grapevine).

At the third meeting, two senior staff turned up and listened intently as Caroline outlined what she intended to discuss at the next meeting, saying that it would be of 'special interest' to everybody. At the fourth meeting, all the senior managers from production and stores attended.

Boldly, Caroline divided the meeting into two groups and sent the stores and the production personnel to separate rooms with instructions to take a couple of hours to fill flip charts with answers to two questions: 'What is the role of the other department in this firm's activities?' and, 'What could they do that would make our department's tasks easier?'

At 11.30 a.m. she brought them back together and they displayed their completed flip charts round the room. She asked each department to report on their discussions.

It didn't take long for the usual angry banter to give way to nervous laughter, because many of each department's statements were the mirror image of the other's. Even the semi-serious and usually provocative but daft statement that stores regarded production as 'the biggest obstacle to an efficient stores', or the equally fatuous assertion from production that 'stores existed to prevent production manufacturing output', only provoked embarrassed laughter and not the usual walk-outs.

Once the managers got the wilder accusations off their chests, they turned with relatively good humour to consider the sensible suggestions that were left on their sheets. For example, stores complained that production people seldom quoted the right parts numbers, which caused them to waste time rechecking before they could search the stacks for the parts. They also told many anecdotes about parts being issued under one number only to be returned later with a requisition for a different number, requiring stores to do twice as much work to issue one item.

Production complained that they seldom knew which parts were available in the stores and wasted a lot of time asking for parts that were on 'resupply'; they gave as many anecdotes about parts being on resupply (unavailable and re-ordered) one minute and 'available to issue' to somebody else a few minutes later.

GET INTO THEIR DRAWERS AND SAVE MONEY!

A CEO of a large insurance company reported that one weekend when the offices were closed, he organised security to open everybody's desk drawers, filing cabinets and cupboards and collect all the surplus office supplies (paper, pens, staples, envelopes, scotch tape, rubber bands, and so on) and sort it into neat lots.

A quick calculation showed many months' supply of stationery – in some cases enough for years! – distributed in furniture outside the official stores, worth many thousands of pounds or 40 per cent of the annual stationery budget. He initiated a campaign to eliminate waste.

He was wasting his time, because two years later the stationery budget had crept up again. The problem was in the store's system and in the staff's 'magpie' habit of always taking more than was needed to guard against stock-outs in the stores just when a print run was needed. He had not addressed the causes of the problem – only its symptoms.

Caroline revealed that a printout of everything that was in the stores, complete with accurate part numbers, arrived from purchasing every morning. Production immediately suggested that this be made available to them for consultation before anybody wrote out requisitions for parts. It would save wasting time requisitioning parts that were listed as 'resupply'. Stores eventually, though grudgingly, agreed to this unprecedented degree of openness if it meant accurate parts numbers would be assured.

What a difference!

To outsiders these changes seem trivial but in thousands of plants across the land, stores and their internal customers continue at loggerheads (for them, as Italians say, 'La lutte continua'!).

Caroline brought about a change in behaviour, not by her line authority (she had none) nor by making appeals to common sense or company patriotism (she saved her breath). First, she sought responsibility for tackling the problem and second, she subtly transformed the people who, essentially, were the problem into the people who became the solution. She influenced the outcome without being dictatorial and in doing so demonstrated her suitability for higher responsibility. She had achieved what nobody had managed before and what nobody thought was possible. Needless to say, Caroline is no longer a junior Materials Manager.

Interestingly, I noticed some months later that stores had taken down the wooden partition with the tiny hatch and had replaced it with large sliding clear glass door-length windows. They were relaxed about production personnel entering the stores to self-search for the parts they needed, including over the weekends or on the night shift, when no stores personnel were present.

In stores, that is a major culture shift.

ACTIVITY 19

Consider if Caroline's approach could be applied in your place of work where there is an intractable dispute.

Not every case where a change in behaviour is required is susceptible to the methods used by Caroline. However, it can be done and something analogous might be attempted where circumstances warrant it. The principle is always that change occurs more surely where the authors of the change want the change to be effected, and when the change is initiated by the persons who will be affected by the change.

Conducting an influencing strategy to achieve behaviour change in those outside your authority is difficult but rewarding. And nothing more clearly demonstrates your suitability for advancement or the healthy state of your influencing skills – if you are successful.

ANSWERS TO SELF-ASSESSMENT TEST 6

1. (a)   No. Exhortation is seldom an effective way to change behaviour.

   (b)   No. Exhortation is seldom an effective way to change behaviour.

   (c)   Yes. However, it's a pity none of your staff have yet shown the initiative themselves to want the responsibility for initiating the search for a change in the way work is carried out in your function.

2. (a)   Perhaps, but it sounds like a lame excuse from somebody who has been brainwashed by too long in the system.

   (b)   Perhaps, but not a conclusion you can jump to without much further investigation (and certainly not an expressible opinion for an influencer!).

   (c)   More than likely. Worth your while to check out, though. Seek responsibility for it as an influencing project.

3. (a)   Yes. But make sure you are successful.

   (b)   Yes. But make sure you are successful.

   (c)   No. She might give the opportunity to someone else.

SELF-ASSESSMENT TEST 7

1. You are very experienced in your domestic markets and you learn of some excellent opportunities for your services in a foreign country, of which you have no experience. This could be just what your business needs. Temperamentally, are you inclined to:
   (a) show cautious interest but not too much enthusiasm?
   (b) show enthusiasm but not too much caution?
   (c) show neither interest nor enthusiasm?

2. You spot a great opportunity for the organisation and believe that nobody else has spotted it yet. This could lead to rapid promotion and great prestige if you could introduce the organisation to the opportunity. Do you:
   (a) keep it to yourself until the next meeting of the board?
   (b) consult with some trusted allies to gauge their reactions?
   (c) send a memo revealing the opportunity to everybody simultaneously?

3. An operation you are running is showing, as yet hidden, signs of drifting into trouble, which unless checked will damage you in your position. Do you:
   (a) seek a move to another operation as soon as possible?
   (b) speak frankly of your concerns to the boss?
   (c) carry on hoping to solve the problem before anybody notices?

CHAPTER 7

Cash is king, invoices are commoner

or why it's risky to seek support

You won't operate for long without having to enlist the support of others for something you want to happen (or not to happen) and you won't operate well, or for long, without being successful more times than you are unsuccessful at mobilising support for your projects.

Notions that you can operate as a 'lone ranger', riding into town as a stranger and, by virtue of your individual genius, achieving all that you want without help from others is pure tosh. Showdowns with powerful individuals, whom you sweep aside on your way to the top in personal gladiatorial contests, barely make it as plots in television soaps and they never make it as career plans.

ON YOUR WAY UP?

A firebrand of a newspaper editor, operating on the usual frantic editorial floor of a tabloid, fired a features editor to hire somebody 'less jaded'. The publicity and the associated gossip did not go down well with the features editor, who took a lower-paid job on another newspaper and suffered the ignominy of the slur that she was 'jaded'.

Two years later, she became editor of the newspaper to which she had moved and, coincidentally, her husband became the boss of the newspaper group that owned the tabloid from which she had been sacked.

The tabloid was now in a circulation slide and the firebrand editor was sacked. She replaced him in a blaze of publicity about his 'jaded editorial loss of direction'.

It pays to remember the adage about being nice to those you meet on the way up because you might meet them on your way down.

The organisations you are likely to join are not full of disparate low life, shifting their allegiances in search of charismatic leaders. Organisations are already structured to serve functions into which you have to fit, and they are staffed by people with whom you have to co-operate for the organisation to achieve its goals.

Organisations, like people, have a history. On the day you join there are many influencing games, some just starting or already under way, and others about to end. Into these competing agendas, you jostle for attention.

ACTIVITY 20

How long did it take you in your current job to spot the ongoing influencing games?

The saloon does not go silent just because you – the lone stranger – walk through the swing doors. You don't achieve mastery of attention by dramatic devices like 'out-shooting' or 'out-punching' the 'baddies' from operations management, or by catching the 'crook' from Research with a fistful of aces in an inter-departmental card game!

To gain influence, you have to secure and maintain the support and co-operation of many others. Gaining support is your most critical strategic objective as an influencer; losing it is decisive.

Put bluntly, without support you won't influence anybody.

But it is somewhat more complicated than this. Winning

support is necessary to win influence, yet winning influence is often a prelude to losing it! Your influence is always under siege.

You build influence to achieve something or stop it happening. Your name is on the parcel. If it goes belly up – the unexpected happens – you go belly up with it. Succeed in garnering support for your project by all means but remember, if it goes pear shaped, so does your support and with it, your influence.

ACTIVITY 21

Can you recall the last time somebody's project slid under the waves along with the person most associated with it?

Don't think influencing skills are a sure-fire way to rise ever upwards in the firmament. You are not operating in an environment that is benign towards you and your interests. You have many rivals and there are many people whom you rival.

There are as many interpretations of what is in the best interests of the organisation as there are people trying to influence it this way or that. Some authorities on influence fail to caution their audiences that what they might believe is the one true certainty about what should happen can just as certainly be overtaken – and overturned – by events.

There are risks in influencing others, which, if your project does not deliver what it promised, will drag down you and your cause.

To make this clear, consider the events following a successful influencing project in a medium-sized construction company in the south of England. Peter, the owner and founder, commercialised a construction method he had invented in the latter years of World War II. By the early 1970s he had built a profitable organisation, Structural Developments Ltd (SDL), specialising in the economical construction of single-storey commercial buildings using an adapted version of his original designs.

Peter was of an age to seriously consider retirement. The senior management team around him had a good combination of experience and ambition for SDL. One of them, George Wright, a key account sales manager, felt, however, that SDL had taken the original product about as far as it could in the UK market and he wanted to explore export opportunities on a much grander scale.

Others, including Richard, Peter's deputy and national sales director, felt that the market in the UK was not yet saturated and he wanted to relaunch the product and take it right upmarket by changing the cladding and doubling the price.

Over the years, SDL had always exported some structures because they were suitable for tropical climates and, because they could be produced in their original economical, no frills, war-time scarcity version, they were approved by the World Bank and other international agencies for projects in developing countries. With this official endorsement they had sold modestly well but SDL had not gone out of its way to expand into export markets.

Broadly then, there were two 'factions' in the management, each circling the other's wagon trains, looking for opportunities to stymie the other and take SDL towards their version of the promised land. On a head count, George was not as well placed as the much respected Richard, who also had close and continual access to Peter.

An Israeli–Arab peace settlement opened up lucrative export opportunities in the Middle East on an unprecedented scale, and was an event of momentous significance for SDL's internal debate. George, who had been forceful in expressing the export strategy for some months, saw this as his opportunity. He visited the Middle East and liked what he saw and heard. On his return, he proposed to Peter that he explore the prospects for contracts to ship construction kits through local Saudi partners.

Peter was enthusiastic and suggested a working party to develop the details, assess the budgetary requirements and assign personnel. George picked a working party with a majority of open-minded, i.e. convincible, people upon whom he could rely to give him full support. He also controlled the flow of information to the board, ensuring that upbeat messages about export prospects were always repeated. He intended to create a situation where he could count on the support of most directors.

By the time Richard, and the managers who preferred a 'home' upmarket strategy, realised what was developing, they were in no position to prevent a 'pilot' project commencing. George totally won Peter over by taking him to Jeddah to meet the Saudi partners he had found (helped by the British Embassy). He did the same with several other managers to 'sign them up' as supporters of his scheme.

He also divided his remaining critics by proposing to export only the upmarket version of the product ('The Saudis can afford it and they will pay top dollar'), ensuring that their departments would benefit from work-in-progress but only if the new strategy was implemented.

ACTIVITY 22

Did you spot this manoeuvre? Foreign travel attracts support by tempting the untravelled with new locations.

George eventually had enough support among the senior managers and on the board to endorse his strategy and within a year SDL was shipping several millions of pounds' worth of construction kits a quarter, and regularly ran recruitment ads in the national press for construction teams to erect SDL's buildings at numerous sites in Saudi. SDL formed a subsidiary, headquartered in Jersey, to manage the entire operation offshore.

George, inevitably, became managing director of the subsidiary and, informally, was spoken of as Peter's successor, displacing Richard, the heir apparent, who remained an unconvinced critic of the export strategy. Richard, remember, went back with Peter to the early days of SDL.

Within two and a half years the Saudi venture rivalled the UK market in total sales and showed no signs of slowing its growth. With these figures in the balance sheet, George was triumphant and became vice-chairman. Richard retired, still not reconciled to the strategy.

At the moment of our greatest advance, we are vulnerable to a crippling counter-blow from the brute course of events.

ACTIVITY 23

Has anything gone wrong for you just when you thought nothing could?

The problem for SDL was the difference between cash received and invoices sent.

George's subsidiary showed it was achieving high sales volume in the number of units sold. The Saudis, however, paid for many fewer units than SDL (Jersey) was shipping. A lag in payments emanating from Saudi developed. At first, the lag was imperceptible but as the months went by, it became very visible. What started as an inconvenience handled by the banks became a cause of great concern because it threatened the financial viability of SDL (UK), the owners and major creditor of the heavily indebted SDL (Jersey).

Eighteen months of worsening debt brought the party to an end.

The Saudi partners assured George, who assured the main board, that there was nothing to worry about because the money they owed would be paid – eventually. These assurances were received with less conviction as the debt mounted towards six months' sales, then ten.

Similar tales of massive indebtedness, affecting other major companies exporting to the Middle East, appeared in the papers. Some European companies reported debts in excess of £100 million. At SDL, the debt stood at around £15 million.

George's position deteriorated weekly. A final visit to Jeddah to come back with payment (any payment) ended in ignominy for George and the closure of the Jersey subsidiary by SDL's main board. SDL (UK) survived – only just – and Peter, facing the prospect of starting again lost his enthusiasm and sold SDL (UK) to a larger rival.

It wasn't something in George's influencing techniques, nor his objective of securing support for his project, that scuppered him. Events put paid to his ambitions.

It could be argued – and has been by Richard – that what happened was bound to happen and that Peter should never have gone along with George's 'madcap scheme' of relying on 'foreigners' to pay their bills. 'I never supported this reckless venture, and never could see it ending in other than tears,' he told me from his place at the trophy end of the golf club bar, where, according to May, his wife, he spends a high proportion of his retirement.

ACTIVITY 24

Have you heard (or said) something similar about a project somebody is about to initiate?

Every influencing project you ever embark upon will be subject to similar criticism by somebody, mostly out of your hearing, and if you take too much notice of your detractors you will not achieve much. Sometimes the detractors are right – your projects are doomed before they begin, or shortly afterwards. That is the unavoidable cost and risk of initiating change and seeking support for the changes you initiate.

Many projects are thought of but few are supported. Of those, some fail and others succeed. None would succeed unless brave individuals took it upon themselves to create an idea, seek support for it and carry it through, once supported.

Be aware of the risks by all means, but if you let your fear of risk hold you back on every occasion – you have a right to aspire to the 'quiet life' – you will remain influenced by those who take risks and you will not become an influencer of those who are congenitally too risk averse to try.

ANSWERS TO SELF-ASSESSMENT TEST 7

1. (a) Yes. Cautious interest is an appropriate behaviour; enthusiasm is an emotion.
   (b) No. This puts you at risk.
   (c) No. No risk, no gain.

2. (a) This is the 'lone ranger' approach. If there is some flaw in the opportunity not yet seen by you, somebody else may not mind pointing out the flaw.
   (b) Yes. They may spot flaws you've missed. They will also respond positively to being consulted on a confidential basis.
   (c) No. Too indiscriminate and combines the risk of (a) with none of the benefits of (b). Might be tried after (b).

3. (a) If practicable, this might be a cynical but wise move. The incomer can take the blame, though, depending on the nature of the problem, some blame will stick. If done in a panic, you will not be absolved from responsibility.
   (b) Probably the best solution: shared problems are halved, and you may not be forgiven for concealing something the boss should know about.
   (c) Next best to (b) and something that will have to be done anyway – by somebody.

SELF-ASSESSMENT TEST 8

1. Complete the following sentence:
   'One good turn deserves . . .'

2. You go out of your way when giving a lift home to a colleague on wet night. A little while later, you ask her to take your calls for 20 minutes while you run a company visitor to the airport. She declines, as she is taking her lunch break in five minutes. Do you:
   (a) shrug your shoulders and ask somebody else?
   (b) resent her refusal to help you after you gave her a lift home earlier in the week?
   (c) determine not to do her any favours in future?

3. Which do you think causes the most aggravation in most people:
   (a) a stranger refusing to help you?
   (b) a friend refusing to help you?
   (c) a person refusing to help you whom you helped in the recent past?

CHAPTER 8

In praise of the ancient verities

or how to avoid resentment

When you influence you deal in the most basic of human behaviours. You realise what makes people tick. You identify the wavelengths they ride upon. And, if you want to be successful, you keep it simple.

Why?

Because if you complicate how you react to people, you will be disappointed with the influence you generate. Trying to influence people in a world in which Miss Goody Two Shoes is comfortable will prove fruitless. For a start, she ain't here (though I am not so sure about her sister, the Wicked Fairy).

Life is not like that. We must take it as it is and ever more shall be.

The reaction of people to events and to other people is conditioned by social evolution. We can put a modern gloss on what they do (including ethics, religion, morality and good manners, etc.,) but we have no reason to believe that fundamentally people react differently to how they always have. Among these reactions lies a prime influencing skill.

GOOD AND BAD TURNS

Let's be specific.

Of the numerous would-be influencers whom I have asked to

complete the sentence 'One good turn deserves . . . ', I cannot recollect anybody being flummoxed by the task.

Admittedly, one or two have hesitated when asked to complete this sentence, 'One bad turn deserves . . . '.

Both statements go together. Good turns 'deserve' good turns and bad turns 'deserve' bad turns. Now, don't blame me for the 'code'. I, like you, learned way back from experience (and a little heavy reading: 'Eye for eye tooth for tooth', says the Old Testament) what bad turns deserve. That is why nobody I've met has too much trouble completing the code of behaviour relating to good and bad turns.

ACTIVITY 25

If you hesitated before completing the statements what was the problem?

You are not asked to endorse the sentiments implicit in the rules – your personal code (or at least your public affirmations of it) may incline you to behave differently on occasion – but no amount of contrary claims can blind you to the fact that, whatever the behaviour code you or others preach, if you do somebody any kind of turn, there is a strong likelihood that some time later they will reciprocate.

'One good turn deserves another' is a universal behavioural rule that has lasted for millennia, because it works. It is part of the history of the human psyche and it is recognised (if not always practised) by everybody. It should become the cornerstone of your influencing activity.

RESENTMENT

Consider what happens when the code is broken when somebody does not reciprocate a good turn. How do you think the person whose expectations are disappointed feels towards the non-reciprocator? (Ignore what the preacher says they should feel; keep to how they are most likely to feel.)

Yes, a word like 'resentment' readily springs to mind.

And why? Because people judge non-reciprocation according to the age-old code that good favours deserve to be returned when it is appropriate, whatever the intentions of the person who did the initial favour.

ACTIVITY 26

The last time you did somebody a good turn, did you think you would get something back for doing it?

Of course, people often do favours with no thought of getting something in return. In one version or another, 'Do unto others as you would they should do unto you' is a guide to conduct urged on us by all the world's main religions and secular codes of ethics.

Your intentions in doing the good turn form *before* the event, not after. They can be as pure as the driven snow – and for many people they truly are – and not a thought may cross your mind that the receiver owes you anything. But reciprocation, or its absence, comes *after* the event, not before. The difference in timing is significant.

You do somebody a favour with absolutely no prior thought of receiving anything in return and then, some time later, you need a favour from him, but he doesn't do it ('as you would want him to do unto you'). He lets you down. He didn't reciprocate. You certainly did unto him (a favour): 'a friend in need is a friend indeed'.

How do you feel? If you feel no resentment, then either you are kidding yourself or you are of divine origin (without being too flippant, people who believe they are of the latter usually overdose on the former).

ACTIVITY 27

How do you know why somebody does you a good turn or favour?

Somebody does you a favour, which being a favour is some-

70

thing that you clearly wanted her to do. She may have done so without thought of your reciprocation. No way can you know for sure what motivated her to do it.

Now, consider the effect on her of you not reciprocating the small favour. Without being psychopathic, you may feel no guilt, but will she feel no resentment? That is the anvil upon which your lack of influence is hammered out.

Not doing people favours wastes influencing opportunities. Not reciprocating favours positively destroys influence over those whom you provoke into resentment.

True, you can risk that people will not feel resentment at your conduct, but don't build your career as an influencer on a disregard for people's proclivities to succumb to the ancient verities. And be aware of the less obvious consequence that if you do not return favours, your concerns are less than worthy of further indulgence.

In the privacy of your conscience your reaction to non-reciprocation is likely to be some degree of resentment, and the intensity of your resentment may be enough to preclude you from doing others small favours (a small price, they might think) but you might decide to go out of your way to do them positive damage ('Hell hath no fury . . . ' etc.).

What is true for you is true for practically everybody else with whom you are likely to interact. Beware – you break the 'good turn' code at your peril!

BAD TURNS

There is worse, of course. Instead of just neglecting to return good turns, you could do people bad turns and for this behaviour you could pay a truly heavy price.

Unfortunately, you have already been negligent in failing to reciprocate good turns and you have had much practice in doing people positively bad turns too.

How do I know this?

71

Because we live in a world where everybody has certain behavioural drives in common, whatever their other differences. If your influence is less than you desire, one cause of this deficit is almost certainly your track record in the good and bad turns code. Fix that and you are on the road to achieving your desires.

How can you fix it?

Simple. If necessary, break the habit of a lifetime and start doing people small good turns. More, make certain you *always* reciprocate for the good turns other people do for you.

What kind of good turns? How many grains of sand are there on the beach?

There are innumerable opportunities to do good turns. So many, in fact, that it is easy to be overwhelmed by just thinking about them.

ACTIVITY 28

List the many small good turns you have done this week for other people. (If you have done none at all, you have a serious influencing deficit to overcome.)

Of course, if you are far too busy, too important and too aware that life is too short to do anything else, your behaviour is predictable and unexceptional. Most people justify their lack of effort on the good turns front with an easy quip, or express a concern that they will be taken advantage of by others. What they can't do so easily is explain their lack of influence.

QUENTIN'S QUEST

Quentin is an influencer who extends his influence almost before the eyes of his rivals. What is his 'secret'? Something that every one of his rivals could do too.

Quentin welcomes opportunities to be 'taken advantage of by others' and, as he can never be sure just who is going to reciprocate when it is their turn to do so, he is never short of people for whom he does good turns. Given the time and opportunity he would do good turns (at least once) for everybody.

What does Quentin do?

Well, say you need a lift across town, or would be thankful for one. Quentin offers you a lift. If you are short of time and would appreciate some help with a mundane task (filing, say), well Quentin will step in and file away. He is passing the post room on his way to a meeting, so he will take your mail and see that it catches the last collection. If your car has a flat tyre Quentin will help you change wheels.

In short, it doesn't matter what the good turn is – or even whom it is for: Quentin is predisposed to help.

ACTIVITY 29

Do you know anybody remotely like Quentin?

Now be clear: this has nothing whatsoever to do with being unassertive, or needing assertiveness counselling, or training to say no without feeling guilty. Quentin is no wimp in these matters. He is as assertive as he needs to be and does not need protection from exploiters. He knows precisely what he is doing when he does good turns: he is piling up that first layer of reciprocal obligations that is the foundation of all effective influencing strategies. Sure, much of his activity is wasted. Sure, some 'smart asses' take advantage of Quentin in the short run, and they realise their mistake too late.

Remember the indissoluble bond between a good turn and its reciprocation.

Let Quentin down and you send him an indelible message. He does not need to throw a tantrum at your non-reciprocation – that would be altogether too crude for an influencer – but as he now knows what you are about, he has an advantage over you: he knows you are part of the chaff and not the wheat.

ACTIVITY 30

How many similar messages have you sent out recently to people whom you need to influence to get something important done the way you want it to be done? How many times in your career(s) have you done bad turns to the Quentins of your world?

The scale and significance of your good turns is a matter of circumstance and context.

Quentin's little favours are quoted only for illustrative purposes. I could complicate the examples with details of Quentin's real job and I would probably embarrass him by doing so, as he plays in a much tougher league and for bigger stakes than most of us. Some of the people he plays with, or against, do not take prisoners except to humiliate them, and he may not take it kindly if I reveal his day job.

The principle Quentin uses is the same, whether the stakes are big or small. The reciprocation he expects is always proportionate: a small good turn deserves a small good turn in response; a big one deserves a big one – and he is adept at handling both. Partly, this is because he is in the habit of doing both and has been for years.

You, on the other hand, may have to start with the small turns because doing big turns without the necessary preparation is risky. By starting small – with everybody and not just those you like – you can enhance the scope of your good turns, in proportion to the reciprocation you experience from the people with whom you deal.

They need to borrow your bicycle? Fine, and if they reciprocate in some proportionate way, double fine. Over the years, this may lead to them borrowing your Spanish villa – though reciprocating by lending you their bicycle for the villa may be a trifle disproportionate, using their shares to support your re-election to the board may be acceptable!

There are no debts like 'good turn' debts.

ANSWERS TO SELF-ASSESSMENT TEST 8

1. 'One good turn deserves another.'

2. (a) You are a very remarkable person if you do (or you are related to Miss Goody Two Shoes).
   (b) A more likely response.
   (c) The most likely consequence.

3. (a) Will cause some aggravation but you will probably be resigned to a stranger's lack of help.
   (b) Will cause more aggravation because friends are expected to help.
   (c) Will cause most aggravation because people are expected to reciprocate if you have done them favours.

SELF-ASSESSMENT TEST 9

1. You are in company and another guest makes a statement that you know to be factually incorrect and with which you strongly disagree. Do you:
   - (a) tell her she is incorrect and that you disagree with her views?
   - (b) confine your comments to her factually incorrect statements?
   - (c) ask her why she holds to her views?

2. You are listening to a colleague expound his well-known views on GM foods, which you have heard many times before. Do you:
   - (a) listen attentively as if you have never heard his views before?
   - (b) listen just enough to keep in touch with his drift?
   - (c) barely listen at all?

3. You are getting to know someone and she asks you a personal question. Do you:
   - (a) decline to answer any personal questions until you know her better?
   - (b) answer frankly?
   - (c) answer guardedly and ask her a similar question in return?

CHAPTER 9

Fishers of men (and women)

or once more with enthusiasm

Speaking is seldom tidy. And there is more than one untidy script
– yours and mine!

Mostly, we do not know how a sentence will end before we
speak and we interrupt our flow with the verbal equivalents of
parentheses, footnotes and appendices. Even the subject changes
and everywhere there are 'ers', 'ums', 'ahs', and 'you knows'. We
get away with grammatical anarchy if our listener is fluent in the
language and its idioms, and co-operates in ignoring them. If you
doubt this, read a verbatim transcript of a radio conversation and
admire your ability to understand the speaker despite her 'abuse'
of the language. Hansard, the UK's official parliamentary record,
is purged of solecisms before it is printed, primarily to protect the
reputation for literacy among MPs.

ACTIVITY 31

Has anybody annoyed you by nit-picking over everything you say
and the way that you say it? (By the way, there is nothing more
irritating than having your grammar corrected, which makes
pedantry a no-no for influencers.)

When listening, you do not parse the speaker's sentences like a
grammarian. You grasp their meaning, usually without error.

Language plays a major part in influencing. The way you use

language makes a difference when you try – and fail – to build rapport with someone (as a trip down memory lane, past all your failed courtships demonstrates). The language of influencing has little to do with your accent. It has everything to do with your understanding of how relationships flower, how they mature and, if you never get the hang of it, how they wither, sometimes before you knew you failed.

So, let's look at three basic influencing behaviours and see where they take us.

LISTEN, STUPID

The first influencing behaviour, ironically, is not about your use of language – it's about the activity of listening to the language of others. It might strike you as odd to refer to listening as an activity but, believe me, if listening is not an activity – if, as for most people, it tends to be passive – you will passively not have any influence. Effective influencers listen carefully. And that requires effort because they have to listen actively.

You listen faster than you talk, leaving you with nothing much to do in the 'long gaps' in conversations. Boredom is inevitable. Your internal dialogue, that conversation with yourself that never shuts up (even when you are sleeping), cuts in. Nanoseconds later you are away in a daydream, physically present but otherwise somewhere else.

You wait impatiently at the end of her sentence before she gets to it. You interpolate what you 'know' she is about to say. Increasingly, you switch off in the gaps and your attention wanders; occasionally you turn up the volume for confirmation of what you expect her to say.

You are not actively listening.

Mostly, you get away with it. Other times, you don't and she accuses you of 'not listening to a word I say'. When anybody accuses you of not listening, beware. Your conduct is matching the uninterest she expects from you and she might find another way to get your attention. Appearing not to listen neither initiates nor sustains relationships.

Listening is much more difficult than speaking, but the rewards are greater.

ACTIVITY 32

Recall the last time somebody accused you of not listening. How common are these accusations?

To influence, listen more than you talk. One simple technique is to use short summaries. Use them regularly throughout conversations to clarify what you are told and to signal, unambiguously, that you are listening. Short summaries are brief, timely and focused. They accompany all influencing behaviours.

Here are three examples of short summaries for active listening:

'So, what you are saying is that . . .'
'Let me get this right. She told you that the Orion contract was behind schedule and that emergency changes need to be instituted this afternoon?'
'Your position, therefore, is that these procedures are illegal and badly drafted.'

Short summaries quote or paraphrase the words the speaker used, allowing the speaker to confirm, clarify or deny what he said and to assert why his views are valid. Short summaries are neither argumentative nor sarcastic. If anything, your short summaries are empathetic – you are a seeker after truth, not an out-of-work member of the Spanish Inquisition. Understanding what the speaker means precedes judging what he says, and not the reverse.

Effective listening requires effort, particularly in the presence of provocation. You may not be interested in what someone means and may disagree strongly with her meaning. Any disagreement with what you hear and you compose a reply before she has finished.

Sometimes, your shaking head, facial grimaces and narrowing of the eyes betrays your feelings. If she is boring, you glance around, desperately looking for someone to relieve your misery and you make token noises, hoping to hurry her to a conclusion.

The result? A loss of influence, or worse, a potential ally transformed into an enemy.

ACTIVITY 33

Recall conversations in which you believed the participants were not listening closely to what you were saying. How did you feel and what, if anything, did you do about it?

Your best reaction on hearing views diametrically opposed to your own is to ask questions. Starting by telling someone that you disagree with his views is no way to influence his thinking. I bet it does not influence yours when he announces that he disagrees with you, especially if he then proceeds to give puny reasons for his disagreement which you can easily and instantly rebut.

Questions are by far the most potent form of handling a disagreement. Ask questions like: What is the basis of your belief in these reports? How did you calculate that number? What is the source of your data? Could you run over the sequence of events again for me?

Disagreements are obstacles between you and the people you wish to influence. Tune into their wavelength if you want to affect their thoughts, feelings and behaviours and influence the decisions they make that affect you. Questioning that reveals how they feel about what you are discussing is far more helpful than argumentative confrontations.

FISHING

At first glance some 'worldly' managers look askance when introduced to fishing. Some (usually male) managers become positively restless when asked to practise 'namby-pamby' behaviours. But, in a remarkable transformation – normally experienced in the environs of Damascus – they become positively besotted with these 'soft' behaviours, once they discover their power.

Most people, when meeting for the first time, establish who they are, what they do, where they come from and where they live. They fish for the other's rock-bottom life story and decide whether to find out more about them. If you decide you want to know more, you fish for supplementary opportunities. If you don't, you make your excuses and leave.

'Where do you come from?'
'Glasgow.'
'I've never been to England.'
'Really?' she says, shrugging her shoulders, and escapes.

Stop fishing and the relationship aborts. But if you discover something, fish some more.

'What does M in your name stand for?'
'McManus.'
'Oh? My mother's maiden name was McManus.'
'Interesting. It's my aunt's maiden name too.'
'Where did she come from?'
'New Jersey, I think.'
'Well that's a coincidence, because my grandad often spoke of his father's uncle, who went to the USA when he was 12 and was never heard of again.'

A coincidence (he is a long-lost cousin) or not (your distant great-uncle drowned on the *Titanic*), the shared name and possible connection prompts more fishing. Uncovering anything you have in common creates an opportunity. Whether to pursue these opportunities is the first (and, alas, sometimes the last) decision in a relationship.

You are more likely to influence someone with whom you have, or can invent, something in common than if you have nothing much in common at all. The theory that 'opposites attract' is best left to iron filings and magnets. With people, total opposites with nothing in common usually make for a lethal combination.

Because the potential for finding common ground is vast, it is remarkable when two people find that they have nothing in common. Those who decide they have nothing in common, mostly see no benefit in making the effort. Even a fish cannot be caught by rod and line unless it opens its mouth.

Beware though the error of desperately interrogating strangers from the moment you meet them. Many people resent over-familiarity at a first meeting and are cautious about revealing great detail about their personal circumstances.

Some people just cannot shut up and, within minutes of meeting, embark on an encyclopaedic account of their life. Presumably they are on medication.

ACTIVITY 34

Select someone of whom you know very little and fish, using supplementary questions. A stranger is ideal, but take care to ensure he/she is safe to fish with (you might send the wrong signal!). And don't forget to listen more than you talk.

ENTHUSING

Do you encourage people to enthuse about a personal interest they have and do you likewise enthuse about your interests? If you do, don't overdo it – you do not want a reputation for being over-enthusiastic about something to which they are indifferent or hostile. Winston Churchill once described fanatics as people who are interested in only one thing and never change the subject.

Identify special interests by fishing – a belief, an opinion, a preference or a shared interest of some kind. By encouraging their enthusiasm you reinforce positive feelings towards you.

To succeed in enthusing you must convey a sense of excitement at their personal interest. An emotionless tone won't energise a manic enthusiast.

'Tell me, what is it like, just before you abseil?'
'What do you like about driving fast cars?'
'How many times did you meet President Putin?

People are often discouraged, either by anticipating mocking reactions or by brutal cut-offs by people uninterested in anybody but themselves. Trying to influence people to support a project without enthusiasm will never get them excited enough to bother to listen. Overtly encouraging people to talk about their special interests – by fishing and then enthusing – contrasts sharply with their normal experience and they notice the difference. You build relationships because you behave differently from those with whom they normally deal.

ACTIVITY 35

Identify people who you know have special interests. When did you last ask them enthusiastically about their interests?

It is more likely that you will influence someone you encourage enthusiastically to elaborate on her special interests, predilections or experiences. If she commences an in-depth account of her special interests within minutes of meeting you, endure it while you evaluate her sense of proportion. The more relaxed she feels about your interest in her interests, the more she is likely to be receptive – in due course – to your influence.

REVEALING

'Confessing is good for the soul' we are told by people who have a vocational, if not a pecuniary, interest in expanding the confessional habit. But whatever its effects on your soul, there is no doubt that revealing relatively intimate secrets to selected individuals is a characteristic of strong relationships.

Relationships in which intimate revelatory exchanges have occurred are stronger than those with only a few or none. Indeed, it is difficult to conceive of a relationship in which neither party knows anything relatively intimate about the other. Not that you should go around revealing all to everybody.

ACTIVITY 36

Do you have any regrets about revealing too much (or too little) to someone?

The paucity of your conscious revealing behaviour is mainly a problem of time and opportunity, as much as a lack of inclination. Revealing takes time and the right circumstances (unless one of you is naïve or over-curious).

Revealing behaviour is not about salacious confessions, nor need it include them (or for that matter exclude them). Your revelations should be much more than your 'name, rank and number'.

I knew someone who had lived with her partner for fifteen years and did not know he had a middle name, nor where he was born, nor that he was alcoholic (even though this was presumably somewhat difficult to hide), nor that he was a deserter from the French Foreign Legion. In fact, she did not know much about him at all. She only realised how little she did know after he had a serious road accident and routine official checks revealed his background.

The main criterion for successful revealing is that what is revealed is not something normally revealed to others. Those with whom you have no relationship – passing encounters – may not get beyond a morning greeting or similar courtesies and perhaps not even these.

People reveal to each other details of their private lives, feelings and hopes. Their revelations are mutually proportionate. Details of who they are, where they come from, how many children they have, how many marriages, their current domestic arrangements, current job circumstances, their sexual preferences and so on, are exchanged as each lets the other enter into private territory in exchange for being allowed into the other's private territory.

Giving your own detailed 'biography' without listening to details of his would be inappropriate, except in anticipation that later he will have a turn to reveal his. To give him no turn at all cuts you off from him, no matter what you reveal about yourself. Revealing one-sidedly signals that you are not interested in him.

Disproportionate revelation in which you 'top' their low-level revelations (age, job, background and circumstances) with high-level revelations about your wildly exotic life and circumstances also signals lack of interest. That is why relationships are difficult to maintain when the people live in distinctly different circumstances.

Revelation as an influencing behaviour should be mutual, proportionate and balanced. It becomes increasingly intimate as it moves from the standard introductory revelations to the non-standard 'confessional' type revelations that are shared only between the closest of friends. People who share their 'innermost secrets' are more likely to influence each other than if they remain virtual strangers.

Of course, some 'secrets' are shared from familiarity – little bits of information are gradually revealed as a result of constant contact. Some 'secrets' are revealed via gossip – third parties retell what they learn to wider audiences than was intended. But relationship-building revelations are slightly different, in that it is not what is accidentally or unintentionally gleaned that characterises the growing relationship, so much as what is intentionally revealed by one person to another.

ACTIVITY 37

With whom among your colleagues have you exchanged

revelations? What do you know about each other that, as far as you know, is not common knowledge?

ANSWERS TO SELF-ASSESSMENT TEST 9

1. (a) No. She will stop listening as soon as you attack her fact-ually incorrect statement or tell her that you disagree with her views. She'll compose her response while you speak.
   (b) Won't make much difference to her defensiveness.
   (c) Yes. She might be right (and you may have made a mis-take); if not, it is better to let her realise her statements are incorrect than for you to try to do it for her.

2. (a) What you should do but I bet you don't.
   (b) Better than (c).
   (c) What you shouldn't do but I bet you do.

3. (a) How do you get to know her better if she doesn't know you better? Part of this is exchanging personal information.
   (b) May not be wise. Try (c).
   (c) Yes.

SELF-ASSESSMENT TEST 10

1. Someone you have recently got to know mentions a minor problem he has. Do you:
   (a) tell him how to solve it?
   (b) seek more information and then suggest how he could solve it?

2. You want to influence someone to support a proposal you have for the next meeting of the budgetary committee. She mentions she needs an increase in the capital budget. Do you:
   (a) ask her questions about why she needs an increase?
   (b) ask her questions about why she needs an increase and then offer to support her?
   (c) ask her questions about why she needs an increase and what are the consequences of her not getting her proposal through, and then offer to support her?
   (d) ask her questions about why she needs an increase and what are the consequences of her not getting her proposal through and then offer to support her if she supports your proposal?

3. You are listening to someone explaining his holiday disaster but what he is moaning about is incomparably trivial compared to your holiday disaster. Do you:
   (a) listen attentively and with sympathy at the obvious distress he experienced, not mentioning your own experiences?
   (b) listen for a time then top his minor disaster with your mega disaster?

CHAPTER 10

In praise of the hippopotamus

or how to win by wallowing

SOLVING PROBLEMS

When somebody has a problem and you know how to solve it, you should share the solution with her.

Yes? Er, no.

Why not? Surely that is what most people would do?

I agree, but what most people do is rarely a safe guide to what an influencer does – if it was, there wouldn't be much point in influencing others because your efforts would be neutralised by everybody else's. And because what most people do does not help your efforts at influencing others, eradicating the habit of mimicking the herd's behaviours will go some way to improving your chances of influencing them.

So, what is wrong with solving other people's problems?

In itself, nothing. But knowing how to solve somebody's problem is not the same thing as choosing the best time to reveal that you can solve it. You see, as with the punch line when telling a joke, or scoring a goal, or making a pass ('coming on to somebody'), it's all a question of timing. Get the timing wrong and you won't be thanked for 'solving' her problem – nor will she laugh heartily at your joke (nor, for that matter, will you find her receptive to your advances!). In fact, you are unlikely to solve the problem for her because her attention has already moved on.

Of course, when you ring an emergency number for the fire brigade you expect them to respond immediately to your distress call. The last thing you want is a prolonged interview about your situation. When the flames are toasting your flanks, you need fire-fighters, not customer satisfaction surveys.

NOT SOLVING PROBLEMS

For the majority of other occasions when you mention your problems – and if you believe you are devoid of problems you ain't real – you do not want them instantly solved. This might at first glance appear to be a ridiculous assertion.

Surely, if you have a problem you do want it solved. It stands to reason. Doesn't it?

Think about it.

For a start, you are fussy about who solves your problems – and if you're not, somebody else might be. If your partner needs a shelf put up, you probably expect that you will be asked to do it, not a stranger (to you) whom she met in a wine bar. (Though, if she is fed up asking you, don't be surprised if your shelf-fitting talents are supplanted – along with much else.)

Also, at any one moment you face a number of problems simultaneously and the one you happen to mention may not be the one demanding an immediate solution, seconds after (or even while) you mention it.

Conversationally, problems are revealed *en passant* while discussing other topics. For example, you mention that your car broke down *en route* to the meeting to discuss a budget revision. If you are anxious to discuss the budget revision, you will not be receptive to a colleague opening with questions about the make of your car, or tales about this little garage she knows that fixes cars cheaply.

What is true for you is true for others; so this is one costly mistake which you should correct.

ACTIVITY 38

Are you an instant problem-solver person? Recall the last time somebody insisted on immediately 'solving' a problem for you. How irritated were you?

GEORGE NEWHOUSE

Take the case of George Newhouse, a would-be influencer, who was ambitious, impatient, and knew how to solve other people's problems. His lack of success wasn't for want of trying, nor for lack of opportunities. He was unsuccessful because of his timing. Not that George is an isolated example. Many others make the same mistake.

George was incapable of resisting the imperative to offer his advice, whenever and wherever the opportunity presented itself. He regarded himself as a good conversationalist, sympathetic to people with problems and manifestly willing to take the time to solve these problems at the slightest hint they existed.

When he met somebody he would fish for where they were from, what they did for a living and their domestic circumstances (this last was a habit he inherited from his famous Italian ancestor, Giacomo Casanova). All pretty straightforward fishing, common at a first meeting where we pigeonhole people according to their relative standing in the pecking order.

There's nothing wrong, of course, with fishing. It's the first (and may be the only) thing you do with strangers, and it's also the opener to conversations with familiar acquaintances ('How's it going Jack?' 'Ça va, Henri?'). Sometimes this purely nominal enquiry about each other's situation reveals that for one of you it is not too good. Now, this is where George pounces, because he is in the instant-remedy business:

- 'A bad cough? What you need is Newhouse's Elixir. It'll soon shift the miseries. Only £5 a bottle.'

- 'Too many meetings? What you need is a Newhouse Time Management System. You'll be amazed at how much time you will have to spare. Only £5 a day frees up half a day.'
- 'Queues waiting for the photocopier to be fixed? What you need is a Newhouse Copier Maintenance Contract. You'll never waste another minute in a queue. Only £5 an hour.'

Get the picture? George is there to 'sell' something and the polite exchange of pleasantries reveals that this person 'needs' what, fortuitously, he wants to sell.

Will they buy? Unlikely.

ACTIVITY 39

In what ways recently have you purveyed an instant solution?

It's no different in principle if George wants to influence a policy. He makes the same mistake: mention a problem and he pounces:

- 'The assessment reports always arrive at the last minute and they are too long to study properly before we make a decision.'
  'That's why you should vote for Henri for comptroller of the budget, to bring some administrative experience to the job. He ran the Westgate Project and was voted the best project leader last year.'
- 'I hope it's a short meeting tomorrow.'
  'Support a continuation on item 8, while we investigate AMP's attitude to disablement and it will be.'
- 'I'm really upset about this decision.'
  'Reverse it at the next meeting by supporting our amendments.'

Sure, there may well be contexts in which such responses are appropriate. Mostly, there aren't.

George's knee-jerk responses show more than his impatience. He shoots from the hip, on sight and without thought. He does not realise how poorly he understands how decisions are made. Not that George sees it this way. He genuinely believes that he is doing fine – even better than fine – because he uses your problem to steer you to one of his solutions. Remarkably, many sales training programmes are as ignorant of how people make decisions as George. They praise the instant sale of products to anybody who hints at a need. It seldom works in the selling of candy bars, yet generations of sales staff go through sheep-dip training in the instant sale and try to apply it when selling big-ticket items like power stations.

Evidence shows that instant selling is ineffective, as you will know from your experience of the opinionated sellers who instantly solve problems you did not know you had, for money you have not got and with liabilities you would rather avoid.

Below-average influencers respond in the manner of pre-programmed sellers. Smell a problem and they salivate like Pavlov's dogs. That ought to be enough for you to sit up straight and take notes.

ACTIVITY 40

When was the last time a pre-programmed seller gave you an instant solution in which you were not interested?

IT DOESN'T WORK

If it ain't working, fix it!

How?

To see why and how, let's use introspection and consider what the instant problem-solver forgets. At any one moment you are beset with many decisions. Mostly, you decide without giving it much thought. You postpone some decisions and move on to others.

Why? Because there are just too many decisions coming at you in an unsorted order. So you sift and sort as you go along.

You're thirsty. Do you stop what you are doing (a decision) and get something to drink (a decision) and, if you do, what do you get to drink (a decision) and where do you drink it (a decision)? While thinking about any one of these decisions, something else might occur to you to interrupt your wavering. How important is it (a decision); what else could I do (a decision); how long will it take (a decision); can it wait (a decision); what happens if I do something else (a decision)? And so it goes on, all throughout your waking hours. Decisions, decisions – Lord save me from decisions!

ACTIVITY 41

Pause right now and count the decisions you have made in the last ten minutes (including those not to do something else).

Add in telephones ringing and faxes slithering across the desk, e-mails hitting your domain; memos piling up; reports to read; coffee to drink; meetings to schedule; itches to scratch and people to see (and some to avoid), plus the daily interruptions of just living, and you become one easily distracted individual.

Ten minutes into a conversation with somebody, you allude to a problem taken from a crowd of your problems, which may be music to the ears of your listener, but not the purpose of your passing allusion. Your listener, however, can solve the problem. So bang! She offers to solve it.

How do you treat her solution? With a 'wow, let's do it'?

Hardly.

You are distracted, remember? More likely, you make your excuses and leave. The last thing you want is the hassle of dealing with her 'solution' to your avoidable 'decision'.

As always, what's true for you is true for others.

Maybe her advice is good. Maybe you should properly consider it. That you don't is a comment on the priority of this one, perhaps minor, problem in the rank order of all the problems trespassing on your attention span at that moment.

WALLOW TOWARDS A SOLUTION

Let's turn now to the hippopotamus and its habits. A wholly relaxed animal, the hippo knows how to get more for his effort. What does the hippo like best? Yes, to wallow in 'glorious mud'. Not that you should wallow in mud – perish the thought! But you should consider inculcating the habits of the hippo in people you hope to influence.

Courtesy of the humble hippo, wallowing can turn your hopes into reality.

The problem of instant problem-solving is that it is no use having a solution if you haven't got the attention of the person with the problem. By the simple act of inducing them to wallow, you increase your chance of success. When someone wallows with his problem, he increases the attention he pays to the problem as surely as a hippo adds to his happiness wallowing in a muddy river. (Have you ever seen a hippo other than grinning while wallowing?)

Consider how George might have induced you to wallow over the delays to the assessment reports. Essentially, George wants to bring these delays further up your personal agenda, preferably to the top of it, so that the subject pushes aside the other distractions vying for your attention.

'The assessment reports always arrive at the last minute and they are too long to study properly before we make a decision.'

'Is that inconvenient?' asks George.

'You bet it is.'

'How do you cope, then?'

'Winging it, to be honest.'

'Does that worry you?'

'Sure it does. I'm not sure that the delays are uninten-
tional because recently, I felt something was not right with
a report, but didn't see what it was until after I got back to
my office and studied the sales figures more closely. It was
obvious when I checked back that they were not as good
as they had predicted in their spring projections, for
which they had secured a £100,000 increase in their
staffing budgets at my department's expense.'
'How did you feel when you found that out?'
'Bloody livid, I can tell you. They had conned the budget
committee and had got away with it and our IT
investment is held back for another six months as a
result.'

And so on. George induces you to wallow, wallow, wallow!

Instead of instantly advising you to vote for Henri for
comptroller of the budget, George induces you to wallow and
recall more details of what happened and how you felt at the time.
Clever! As you recall your feelings, they grab your attention. You
feel them again. Even the physiological changes – in heart rate,
perspiration, body language – you experienced at the time return.

'Bloody livid' feelings become real again as you feel your anger.
You are also far more susceptible *at that moment* to suggestions as
to what to do about the problem, provided – and this is George's
pièce de résistance – he gets you (not himself) to say in your own
words what it is worth to you to resolve your problem.

'In what ways would you benefit from having these reports
delivered in good time?'
'For a start, we might have saved £50,000 at least from our
staffing budgets if we had spotted the sleight of hand they
pulled before the meeting.'
'On what would you have spent the money?'
'Enhancing senior programmers' pay and recruiting a
graphic designer.'

And that is where George springs his solution of voting for Henri as comptroller. He has your full attention, you are still brooding over the 'theft' of your budget, you are spending the £50,000 in your mind and, above all, you want something done about it.

If you say:

'I hope it's a short meeting tomorrow'

how should George respond? Well, by inducing you to wallow in the reasons why you hope for a short meeting. That makes you feel more anxious about the duration of the meeting and, the more anxious you feel, the more receptive you will be to his solution of curtailing the meeting by supporting 'a continuation on item 8 on AMP's attitude to disablement'.

Likewise, you reveal:

'I'm really upset about this decision.'

Isn't it better for George to find out why you are upset by getting you to wallow in what is upsetting you? Of course it is! Going straight to the solution leaves you to make a decision before you delve below your surface emotions and wallow in them.

Get the idea?

Engage people in an empathetic probing of incidents, problems, moods and doubts and induce them to wallow in them. Then get them to state in their own words the benefits of solving the problem and finally, offer your viable solution.

ANTI-WALLOWING

Generally, people are delighted when they wallow. Perhaps this is why, once its purpose is appreciated, I have never experienced the slightest difficulty in enthusing hard-boiled managers to practise wallowing. Many claim to be pleasantly surprised at what it does for them. Wallowing has many applications in influencing, persuading and the management of meetings. It is also widely used between friends, though few probably call it wallowing. For that reason, wallowing is barely mentioned by management gurus.

Many people do the opposite of inducing wallowing. They cut people off just as they get into a wallow. When asked why they do this, they say that the idea is 'pointless' and 'time-wasting gossip'. They could not be so wrong if they threw excrement at the people they need to influence.

Take some everyday examples of anti-wallowing behaviour.

Barbara tells you she had an awful journey to work. You barely listen to her, or worse, you top her tale of woe with your own wallow about your journey to work, which you insist was much worse than hers. You don't induce her to elaborate on her awful journey, you don't make empathetic noises and you don't fish for her feelings about her stress – you don't, in short, encourage her to wallow.

By killing Barbara's wallow, you kill an influencing (and any other!) opportunity.

Mustafa tells you he cannot process your data because he is up to his ears testing software for the Omega project, which is behind schedule. You challenge his priorities, cast doubt on the Omega project, tell him how important your data are and eventually storm off in high dudgeon.

You don't listen sympathetically to his problem and you don't encourage him to wallow on the 'unreasonableness' of the Omega people. You do not empathise with him. Letting Mustafa wallow, you believe, would be to waste time. And you still don't get your data, either this time or (unremarkably) in future when you have a similar urgent need for his services.

You believe that Avril needs your air-conditioning services but she is uninterested in your pitch. Your aircon, you tell her, is much more reliable, runs more efficiently, has separate controls in each room, can adjust automatically through sensors to the number of people entering or leaving a room, and above all is cheaper to run than the system her predecessor installed. You told her (repeatedly) about your product after she showed indifference. When pressed, she shrugged her shoulders and said, somewhat aggressively, that she had another appointment.

What went wrong?

You failed to let Avril wallow in her unhappiness and merely tried to sell her something. In short, you did not earn the right to solve her unhappiness. You can rationalise your failure with the rap line: 'Not every pitch makes you rich', but remember, there's something wrong if a pitch don't make you rich.

Wallowing is too easily dismissed as self-indulgence, and as easily – and frequently – discouraged. People in a hurry, we are told, have no time to waste listening to someone 'moaning'.

Right? Wrong!

ACTIVITY 42

How many times do you terminate conversations before you allow the other person to wallow? Now consider the consequences of your behaviour.

If you cut people off before they wallow to curtail the boredom of their moaning, it undermines your relationships. Interestingly, 'intellectuals' despise other people's wallowing (though not their own). There is no more awesome sight than a professor who professes she has 'no time for moaning minnies', in a full-throat wallow at a budget meeting. The absence of shared wallowing probably explains 90 per cent of the reasons why you lack influence.

ACTIVITY 43

Search for an opportunity to induce a wallowing sequence with someone.

Actively listen for a problem they have experienced recently. Fish with wallow questions, such as:

- What is the problem?
- How did it affect you?
- How did you feel at the time?
- How did you adjust to the problem?
- How would you benefit if the problem was solved?

So induce some wallowing and become a better influencer!

ANSWERS TO SELF-ASSESSMENT TEST 10

1. (a) No. Instant solutions are not treated seriously.
   (b) Better than (a).

2. (a) Good start but not sufficient.
   (b) Better start, but still not sufficient.
   (c) Even better but still not sufficient because it is not linked to what you want.
   (d) Much the best.

3. (a) Yes. Do not 'top' other people's wallows.
   (b) Definitely not.

SELF-ASSESSMENT TEST 11

1. If you know that most people call heads and not tails in a coin toss, what do you expect a person to call when you toss a coin to allocate something important to the winner:
   (a) heads?
   (b) tails?

2. You give an arbiter your final position in a dispute over a price and reckon that there is a 75 per cent probability that the arbiter will choose your bid. What probability is there that the arbiter will choose the other person's different bid?
   (a) 25 per cent.
   (b) 75 per cent.
   (c) 50 per cent.

3 If you are cut off suddenly during an important phone call, do you:
   (a) call the person back immediately?
   (b) wait for him to call you back?

CHAPTER 11

The problem with other people

or how to advance in the other direction

You are invited to participate in an experiment in which you have to fly to Paris and choose a place to meet someone, whom you don't know and cannot contact, at exactly 12 noon the day after tomorrow. If you choose exactly the same place for the meeting as the other person (who doesn't know you either), you will each receive $100,000.

Where would you choose to be in Paris at 12 noon?

The Eiffel Tower, the Louvre, the Hôtel des Invalides, Notre Dame, the Arc de Triomphe, or somewhere else?

Your problem is that whatever method you use to make your choice, it must correspond exactly with the unknown person's choice. Otherwise, neither of you gets $100,000.

Similar mind games illustrate the superiority and the fragility of rationality in decision-making.

The results illustrate that unfamiliarity with the city tends to drive participants to choose prominent landmarks (Sydney's Opera House, London's Big Ben, Rome's Colosseum, Washington's White House, Peking's Tiananmen Square, and so on).

ACTIVITY 44

Where would you meet in the city in which you live? Try the mind game with a friend.

Conversely, the more familiar the participants are with a city (the one in which they live, for instance) the more widely they disperse their choices and the greater the difficulty of securing positive co-ordination of pairs of players.

When pairs of players, because they reason differently and irrespective of their familiarity with the city in the game, choose different places to meet, verbal conflict (sometimes quite heated, too) breaks out between them.

'How could you choose Café Danton in the rue du Bac and not the Eiffel Tower?' declared one angry participant (and, remember, the 'prizes' in a workshop are imaginary too!), to which she replied: 'Because I once had a romantic meal in Café Danton!' She had, of course, completely missed the point that her partner, who was dependent on her rational choice for his share of the (small) prize, had to make the same choice she made and that, because they were strangers, he had no knowledge of her long-standing romantic memories. Perhaps even her former lover has forgotten her and the Café Danton!

When a valued outcome (your life could be at stake) is frustrated by the reasoning process of another, accusations of irrationality surface, and quickly too.

The mind game replicates real-life clashes between people who behave differently from what is expected.

In the UK, you are expected to drive on the left and in France on the right (in Greece, however, the locals drive down the middle of the road and only pass on the right!). It is always safer not to disappoint the expectations of co-drivers.

If there is a strong expectation that someone will behave in a certain manner, then we consider it 'rational' to behave according to our expectations and 'irrational' if they surprise us. So when people do not behave as expected, we abuse them for being 'stupid', 'illogical' and 'irrational'.

WHEN I SAY THE BACK DOOR, I MIGHT MEAN THE FRONT DOOR

Consider a trivial domestic incident which still rankles years later.

Clive dropped his mother-in-law off at the rear entrance to a large department store and, because of the parking laws, agreed to return and pick her up in twenty minutes, giving her plenty of time to exchange something she had bought the day before.

So when he returned to the rear entrance at the appointed time, he was surprised to find no sign of mother-in-law. He waited for five minutes, then drove round the block and returned. Still no sign. He repeated this process several times for thirty minutes before he gave up. He couldn't leave the car to look for her as an unattended vehicle was bound to be towed.

To drive home he had to pass the front of the shop. And there she was!

She angrily demanded to know where he had been, as she had been 'waiting for ages in the cold'. He as angrily asked her why she was waiting at the front of the store and not the back as they had arranged. She replied, in a tone admitting no argument, that as she would have to climb stairs to go to the back entrance, she stepped out of the front door, because it was on the same level! No amount of argument, logic or rational explanation shifted her from the view that Clive should have known she was at the front door; and, she added contemptuously, 'and you a professor!'

That is the problem with other people. They think differently from us.

We think – to our own satisfaction, at least – that our conclusions are logical, given the circumstances. Many an argument begins with a difference of perception on what should be done in a given situation.

You arrange to meet someone before going on elsewhere with them and they are late. Do you keep on waiting until they arrive at the meeting place or do you go on to the event, leaving them to catch up?

You are on the telephone and the line disconnects. Do you ring them back or do you wait for them to ring you back?

ACTIVITY 45

What examples can you recall of apparently irrational behaviour by someone?

What happens when it's a matter of life or death if an arrangement breaks down, leading to a very unpleasant detention by people who ignore the Geneva Convention on prisoners of war?

You are sent on a mission behind enemy lines with important intelligence on the time and place of a high-level meeting of enemy leaders. You are dropped into the territory within 10 miles of the meeting place and must link up with the nearest SAS trooper, who has the weapons necessary to undertake a surprise attack on the meeting but who doesn't know the location of the meeting.

The problem is that there was no time to brief you or the trooper before your rendezvous. Each knows that the other will be in the approximate area and that he will have to meet quickly, as the area is filling with enemy troops sent to guard the meeting.

Suppose the terrain has a meandering river on the southern boundary and otherwise consists of an undistinguished sand plain with a small building at its centre. It's dark and you do not know if the building is occupied by enemy soldiers.

Got the picture? OK, where would you rendezvous? You cannot wait until daylight, nor use signal flares. If caught by the enemy you will be tortured, perhaps to death and certainly into permanent disability.

People given this mind game choose variously and sometimes argue with passionate ingenuity for their chosen 'solution'. However, it's no use your having a perfect solution if your compatriot chooses another one. That way you'd end up in the 'Baghdad Hilton'! If you don't choose the same solution, you can conduct seminars on rational decision-making while semiconscious during the torturer's rest breaks.

Rationality – or what passes for rationality – is the most common word used by people to describe their influencing method. Yet, what is rational to one person may not be rational to another, and your reliance on rational methods of decision-making is often compromised. Partly, this is because rational choices work best when they affect only ourselves. They are far less effective when we have to interact to make rational choices with somebody else. Indeed, workable scientific models of rational choice are designed for individuals only and not for pairs or groups, yet people do not seem to be aware of the distinction.

Descartes, the French philosopher, rationally concluded 'I think, therefore I am', but he would not have been remotely rational if he had asserted: 'I think, therefore you are.'

It should not surprise you that when people are questioned, they claim frequently to use rational arguments to make their cases. Nobody likes to admit to being other than rational or polite or respectful, so they don't!

In practice – from observation – people certainly believe they are rational. In fact, so sure are they that they respond to rejection by repeating the same case over and over again. It's a bit like the foreigner who can't speak the language, who keeps repeating until she is shouting, as if the repetition and shouting will eventually make her bemused listener comprehend her meaning.

If people are rational, how do they come to different conclusions? It can't always be the case, surely, that you are rational and everybody who disagrees with you is irrational?

This takes us back to the mind games.

Clearly, people who come to different conclusions must start from different premises. We don't all see the same problem – or the world we share – from the same perspective. We have different interests and we bring our perceptions of these to our work.

UNITED WE FALL, DIVIDED WE <u>STAND</u>

Common experiences, and even common objectives, provoke different interpretations of what should be done. People in the same organisation often have very different interpretations of what is the best course for the firm.

Accountants prefer no stocks of work in progress and no warehouses full of unsold products; production favours large production runs with unchanging specifications; sales people prefer large stocks of product in every conceivable variation just in case a customer wants a unique specification, and every department – there are no exceptions – wants a larger share of the budget, because it interprets its own role as central to the objectives of the organisation.

Influencers, who develop their cases from their own perspective, no matter how rational their arguments, are bound to conflict with others who hold to different perspectives, even if they subscribe to similar standards of rationality.

Your own perspective is as good a place as any from which to start but, if you want to influence somebody else, it is a poor place to remain. Presumably, you want to influence others because they are important to your preferred outcome. You need them as allies, or at least as neutrals, not enemies.

When influence comes down to a head count, you need more heads on your side than on the other guy's.

The inescapable conclusion is that you will be more effective in influencing someone else when you address that person's sense of what is rational and not your own. This, of course, means overcoming the habits of a lifetime! To recast your influencing message into the mind-set of the listener requires that you thoroughly understand that person's way of looking at the world and their place (and yours) in it.

You must become outward looking and not a prisoner of your ego. Not for the last time, I remind you that you will serve your own ends best by serving the ends of others. It's not your world through your eyes that counts; it's their world through their eyes that matters.

Seeing 'their world through their eyes' is more than just a pithy saying. It requires more from you than 'stepping into their shoes', because their shoes only go on your feet, which is a long way from your eyes (despite the deluded ravings of 'emotional intelligence' gurus). This leaves you still seeing *their* world through *your* eyes. You soon revert to seeing your world through your eyes when what you 'see' in their shoes doesn't work.

ACTIVITY 46

Who among your colleagues has an obviously different sense of rationality to you? Think of some instances of his or her, to you, irrational behaviour.

If you want to persuade run-of-the-mill accountants to support your proposals you had better cast your case in the cautious language preferred by accountants and not the language associated with high risk seekers.

Breaking into production runs to produce short batches becomes a 'technical challenge' not an indifference to the economics of high output, or a slur on engineering competence. In similar vein, you present low wages as 'employment opportunities', boring activity as 'challenges', receiving boring people as a 'saintly penance', dead ends as 'special projects', and selfish concerns about WIIFM? – 'what's in it for me?' – as selfless considerations that ask:

'what's in it for them?' (WIIFT?).

We call this 'reframing'.

ACTIVITY 47

Reframe some statements common in your line of work.

This means presenting your verbal picture in a way that the viewer understands and appreciates, and in language that appeals to that person's values. It's much like the cliché of the difference between the bottle being half full or half empty, that indicates whether you are a pessimist or an optimist.

In a B-movie, a US Marine recoils from his sergeant's order to go back the way they have come: 'You mean we're gonna retreat, Sarge?' 'Retreat! Hell no, we're just advancing in the other direction.'

ANSWERS TO SELF-ASSESSMENT TEST 11

1. (a) Yes. It is rational to assume people will do what experience shows they normally do but beware: a minority are known to call 'tails'.

   (b) Not unless they subscribe to 'tails never fails'. You would be taking a gamble if you do. If the outcome is important to you, relying on what people are supposed to do may lead to disappointment.

2. (a) According to the 'rules' of probability you are implying $(1-0.75) = 0.25$, but this conflicts with rationality because why should the other bidder put forward a bid that has only a 25 per cent chance of being chosen?

   (b) A bid could have any level of expected probability in the rational mind of another rational bidder but where the two bidders have conflicting expectations of probability (both expect to win with 75 per cent probability, say) they are both being irrational!

(c)   Most likely.

3. (a)   What if he is trying to call you back and the lines are engaged?
   (b)   What if he is waiting for you to call him back?

SELF-ASSESSMENT TEST 12

1. You are chastised by a close colleague for not having the test results on some software completed as you had promised. You explain that some key personnel have been struck by flu and one other broke her leg on a skiing holiday. Your colleague – with whom you have worked closely to enhance your section's budget and with whom you thought you had friendly relations – brushes aside your explanations, suggests you divert two programmers off their current project, tells you two of her staff will join you that afternoon to supervise the team and warns you that if you do not co-operate fully to finish the work by the weekend you will lose her support. Do you:
   (a) tell her to get her tanks off your lawn?
   (b) say 'OK – and thanks for the suggestions'?
   (c) wonder why she is so antagonistic to you given your honest explanations?

2. 'You will get absolutely nothing from me unless and until I get something from you.' Would you describe this statement as:
   (a) aggressive?
   (b) assertive?

3. You need support for a proposal and a close ally announces that he may not attend the next meeting of the budget sub-committee as he is playing golf. Do you:
   (a) express barely concealed outrage that he could be so irresponsible?
   (b) plead with him to change his plans?
   (c) tell him to change his plans or lose your support on something specific that is important to his department?

CHAPTER 12

When push comes to shove

or how to step up the pressure

Harsh exchanges between strangers are not easily tolerated, whereas long-time partners often endure quite outrageous behaviour – as you will know if you listen to partners wallowing at the behaviour of their 'significant other'.

Influencing behaviour can be pushy as well as all 'sweetness and light'. But only with long-term allies. If push comes to shove, be careful whom you push. If he can't take a nudge, you had better not push – in which case, shoving is out of the question.

When the relationship is strong enough, you push your preferences on to people. The robustness of the relationship absorbs your pushing. Push behaviours are seldom successful with virtual strangers.

Influence is built over time and is severely weakened, sometimes totally destroyed, through pushing before you pull. Pushing people with whom you have no relationship is impractical. You come across as arrogant, presumptuous, threatening and 'unbalanced'. Hence, pushing presumes an investment in building a relationship through prolonged exchanges of pulling.

Taking steps to improve your relationships through pulling is a necessary precondition for influencing them by pushing. In short, you must earn the 'right' to push.

Push behaviours include:

reasoning – using a rational argument to justify a decision;
suggesting – making general recommendations;
asserting – identifying the 'correct' decision;
coercing – compelling someone to take a course of action.

The four push behaviours appear deceptively normal for many managers. They are what you do every day – which is part of the problem. Inappropriate behaviours are counterproductive and, dangerously for influence, some people resent and react against the careless use of push behaviours.

ACTIVITY 48

Have many people recently reacted negatively to the way you spoke to them? Were you accused of an aggressive tone, or abrupt language or disrespectful gestures when, in your view, you merely told them to do what they were supposed to do?

Some managers claim that they do not feel comfortable when contemplating practising push behaviours.

REASONING

Rational reasoning is highly regarded in the West, where there is a strong prejudice towards rationality in managerial theory. In argumentative discourse, logic is assumed to be superior to subjectivity. From a given premise, a logical conclusion follows. Any other conclusion is false and logically should be rejected.

'It stands to reason that if we cannot sell in your territory then you cannot sell in ours.'
'On the basis that you wish to impose an inhibition on me writing a book on the same subject for another publisher, logically I must require you not to publish another author's book on this same subject.'

'There is no logic in me accepting prices below my costs of production.'

Asserting that a decision is based on logical reasoning bestows legitimate authority on it. For example, 'The numbers are neutral' and 'We must always submit to the evidence'.

A manager's capability for logical analysis is a powerful tool in disputes on what should be done. When 'you can't argue with the facts', the other person's role in the decision is secondary not primary, because the facts exist independently of both of you. And when you insist that they 'set emotion aside', you diminish their discretionary influence. Dismissing a contribution as emotional or illogical is usually sufficient to discredit it. Hence, this is a frequent charge against contributions with which we disagree, and the basis for the current fad for fighting against narrow rationality in decision-making by evoking the benefits of 'emotional intelligence'.

No discussion on rationality can neglect how rationality is manipulated by those anxious to claim high authority for the decision they prefer. In abstract principle, a rational decision is meritorious in its own right; in practice, claims to rationality may be spurious.

ACTIVITY 49

How many managers do you know who claim to make rational decisions? How many of them demonstrate formally how they arrived at their rational decision?

SUGGESTING

Suggestions are the 'softest' of the four push behaviours. Suggestion is different from advice in that anybody can offer advice (which is mostly ignored), whereas in influencing, a suggestion presumes a relationship in which the suggestion is freely sought and legitimately offered. There is confidence that it will be seriously considered. The likelihood of the suggestion being implemented depends on the strength of the relationship.

> 'Have you thought of contracting out these services?'
> 'In my view, a request for compensation is best backed by a lawyer's writ.'
> 'Pick whom you want but I think you would be better with Morag in that post, not Michael.'

Suggesting behaviour is not an offer of impersonal and disinterested advice. You have a direct interest in the outcome and your suggestion aims to achieve your preferred outcome. So when strangers ask for advice on the shortest route to the docks, you are indifferent if they heed or ignore you. In suggesting that your colleagues should support the building of a new dockyard, you have a direct interest in whether they do and are disappointed if they choose another project instead.

Your confidence in your relationship with a person to whom you feel free to make suggestions is dependent on your confidence that they will heed what you suggest.

ACTIVITY 50

Reflect on the number of suggestions you made today to colleagues.

ASSERTING

Asserting is a step up from the right to make general suggestions to someone (with an expectation that these will be acted upon). Asserting that this or that is the correct decision for someone to make implies a complex relationship. A stranger making an assertion may be ignored; a close ally will not.

> 'You must stand up to Linda on this issue.'

'You should not go on that concert tour if you are to retain your standing.'

'If you don't fight back now, you will pay for it over and over again.'

Assertive behaviour is not meant to be ambiguous. You know where you are with assertive people. The language they use is clear, to the point and devoid of shambolic rambling.

In appraisal interviews, for example, it is necessary to be absolutely clear when stating what the interviewees must do to achieve a satisfactory rating. Praise for their achievements is matched by specific details of where they have fallen below standard and what they must do about it. If something less than assertive behaviour is used, the sub-standard behaviour has less chance of correction. Advice that 'you must try harder' is less valuable than the specific targets you must reach in attendance, or in time-keeping.

Evasive decision-making styles are well short of assertiveness, because they use language like 'on the one hand and on the other', which invites uncertainty about what must be done.

COERCING

Coercive behaviour works in robust relationships and provokes resistance in weak ones. It is an extreme form of influencing behaviour. You pressurise the person to act in a specific manner in pursuit of your goals. The form of compulsion varies from a direct instruction ('Vote for the rejection of the minutes of the board meeting') to a threat ('If Harry wins the vote because you fail to support me, then I will not support your promotion').

The difference between asserting and coercing is that asserting is still advice ('you must stand firm') and coercion is a command ('stand firm, or else').

Coercion indicates some degree of power. Relationships give power to the influencer and, as noted, partners behave towards each other in ways that would not be tolerated in the absence of a relationship.

ACTIVITY 51

Have you been coerced recently? Have you coerced recently?

Examples of altercations between domestic partners come to mind (observe how spouses treat each other compared to how they treat lovers). Similarly, interpersonal tensions between politicians in the same fraternal party are often fraught (some members of the Cabinet cannot bear to be in the same room with certain of their colleagues).

> 'Go to the match, but I will not be here when you get back.'
> 'Remember, hell hath no fury like a woman scorned and not supporting Amelda on this vote will cost you dear.'
> 'If you can't stand the heat, get out of the kitchen.' (Or, in a memorable gaffe that cost a prominent British politician his power base in the local constituency when he antagonised critics among women members: 'If you can't stand the heat, get back to the kitchen!')

Coercion is a complex relationship behaviour, hardly different from bullying and intimidation. It may be willingly accepted, or as vigorously resisted if some indeterminate line is crossed. Coercion is often accepted out of a sense of obligation, but it is fiercely resisted when it humiliates or exploits the coerced and they have a viable option to switch sides.

COMBINING PULL AND PUSH BEHAVIOURS

While it is true that pull behaviours are associated with the tentative stages of a growing relationship and push behaviours are associated with more robust stages, there is no strict linear one-way progression from fishing to coercion.

You combine and sequence pull and push behaviours throughout a relationship to suit circumstances. Sometimes you fish, sometimes you wallow, sometimes you suggest and sometimes you coerce. You are unlikely ever to exhaust the incidence of the repetition and elaboration of mutual revelations. As for wallowing, variants of it will be exercised sometimes with enthusiasm and sometimes in sadness (at the content).

Push and pull behaviours have subtle variations and can be combined in many ways too. The key is to recognise how to behave to achieve the results you seek from the relationship. Concomitantly, it is necessary to know when the circumstances dictate that certain behaviours are not appropriate. There is nothing to be gained from push behaviour when pull is called for, or from pull behaviour when a more direct push is required.

ANSWERS TO SELF-ASSESSMENT TEST 12

1. (a) Not if you want to keep her support.
   (b) Yes.
   (c) Probably, but this should make no difference to (b).

2. (a) No. Its content is assertive – defined as securing your rights without trespassing on someone else's. It can be said aggressively – as can almost any sentence.
   (b) Yes. Knowing the difference is important and many managers benefit from learning that there is a difference.

3. (a) Not if this is all you do.
   (b) A weak move with a strong ally.
   (c) Yes – pressure is more likely to succeed in these circumstances.

SELF-ASSESSMENT TEST 13

1. Your neighbour, a teacher, is bending your ear about the lack of spending by the government on education and how this will damage the future of young children who will be inadequately taught the things they need to know for careers in the modern world. Does this suggest:
   (a) that your neighbour wants a pay rise?
   (b) that your neighbour is worried about the education of young children?
   (c) that your neighbour wants to spend more money on educating children?

2. A surgeon, interviewed on television about hospital spending restrictions, stated that it was immoral for money to enter into considerations of health. Did he mean:
   (a) that there is no limit to the resources that a moral society should spend on health provision?
   (b) that as a moral person he would be prepared to work as a surgeon without considering the amount he was paid?

CHAPTER 13

The currencies of influence

or how to behave selflessly

Adam Smith, Professor of Moral Philosophy at Glasgow University, published *The Wealth of Nations* in 1776, the year when George Washington and his pals went head-to-head with the Redcoats.

Smith understood influencing and you would do well to apply his advice with gusto. He advised that your best chance of persuading the 'butcher, the baker and the brewer' to supply you with your dinner was to appeal to their self-interest and not to their charity.

Against such sensible advice, some prejudiced scribblers leapt on Smith's reputation with outrageous disregard for the ordinary meaning of words. They accused him of advocating selfishness as the guiding principle of human activity!

How wrong can you get?

They confuse being 'selfish' with the altogether different word, 'selfless'. Literacy is not their strong suit. Smith, for certain, did not advocate selfishness as a vocation. He merely noted, from observation (a wholly reputable source), that people who want the essentials for a good dinner would be wise to remember that the butcher, the baker and the brewer have interests too.

ACTIVITY 52

Imagine if everybody relied on everybody else's charity. Where would the wherewithal for everybody to be charitable come from?

Whether people should be motivated by their self-interest is not relevant — if you had to wait for your dinner until everybody denied their self-interest, you would face a long (and hungry) wait. While a few can rely on charity, thousands of millions cannot.

Smith, sensibly and sensitively, took people as they were and enjoined his readers to address themselves to other people's interests when in pursuit of their own.

What did Smith observe?

Simply, that you are more likely to serve your own interests by addressing yourself to the interests of those who have what you want. In short, *serve others to serve yourself*! Now, that ain't an immoral philosophy is it?

The alternative of expecting others to serve you is cynically exploitative, as well as naïve and truly selfish. Persons subscribing to the immoral philosophy of living off others are likely to be disappointed.

For most people, interests are the final arbiter of their behaviour. The influencer who follows Smith's advice is more than casually interested in other people's interests, because other people's interests drive their behaviour while they serve our own.

And what is true for you, is true for other people who wish to influence you. The most useful question, therefore, is always: 'What are their interests?' If you don't know their interests, you know nothing about those whom you would influence. Your chances of success are like throwing dice.

People, though, while conscious of their broad interests, do not always realise the consequences. Their multiple interests may conflict and they may need to be reminded of this before they jump to a decision.

CHECK THE BIG PICTURE 1

'Sure, this proposal would create some desperately needed new jobs in Aberdeen, but these jobs are outside the manning agreement we signed with the employers last year and they are the thin edge of an anti-union wedge that will eventually destroy jobs in Glasgow. Are fifteen new jobs in Aberdeen worth 3,000 old jobs in Glasgow?'

Sometimes people are embarrassed by their interests. They then find other spurious, though plausible, reasons to block something happening against their interests. You see, it isn't over just because you discover their interests.

CHECK THE BIG PICTURE 2

'OK. So you demand a 20 per cent pay increase for the drivers. We cannot pay that much. You insist we can and a strike will commence at midnight if we don't. So let me make it clear. Should you pursue your impossible pay objective with a strike, corporate headquarters in Geneva will close the business. This is not an idle threat to dissuade you from pursuing a pay rise. This depot contributes less than 0.2 per cent of the company's European turnover and less than nothing to the company's net profit – we barely break even on our fixed assets. Now, which is more important to you – an impossible pay rise or having a job? Let me know, so I can fax corporate headquarters – and then get on the phone to look for another job.'

Everybody who ever 'sells' ideas learns this truth one way or another: people 'buy' what you're selling if what they buy serves their interests. If it doesn't, they don't.

ACTIVITY 53

Think of any idea you suggested recently that was not accepted. What interests of the other person did it address? Which interest of yours did it address?

It doesn't matter that the idea you sell is intangible, like a policy, your support, the reversal of opposition, neutrality, or them not striving too officiously to prevent what you want to happen. It could be anything: from a notion to a gesture, from a symbol to a slogan.

Interest-based influence is powerful because addressing someone's interests is always – there are no exceptions! – the gateway to them addressing yours. Start from their interests, not yours, and you are unlikely to go far wrong.

Smith, of course, referred exclusively to cash transactions. Each person explicitly negotiates to exchange something (bread, meat and beer, say) in exchange for money. The dynamics of negotiating are fully explored in my companion book, *Everything is Negotiable!* (Arrow), and I shall say nothing more about explicit trading here.

In influencing, the exchange is different in two ways.

The first difference is that influencing transactions are implicit. There is no formal contract stating each party's obligations and the enforceable penalties for non-performance.

The second difference is that while influencing transactions also involve 'currencies', these currencies are not in the form of tangible cash. Influencing currencies are intangible. They consist of 'services rendered', 'sentiments expressed', 'commitments made' or 'obligations fulfilled'. They take numerous forms and different people trade in different currencies.

Influencing currencies at the generic level include, but, as the lawyers say, are not limited to, those in Figure 13.1. We shall run through some of these currencies quickly to get the flavour of their possible roles in your influencing.

125

People prefer some currencies to others. You must identify correctly which, of the currencies available, might be best received by the particular individual you wish to influence.

Examples of active trading in some of these currencies follow, with the reminder that in influencing, unlike in negotiation, the 'donor' of the currency is not explicitly trading what she gives for what she wants from the receiver. There is no direct connection between the acts of the donor and reciprocation by the receiver. All influencing transactions are indirect: like good turns, they are traded in the expectation that *in due course* there will be some kind of reciprocation from the receiver (with similar consequences for the receiver of a currency as when a good turn is not reciprocated).

FIGURE 13.1 SOME POPULAR INFLUENCING CURRENCIES

Support the vision
Create excellence
Apply ethics
Release resources
Offer assistance
Publicly support
Respond quickly
Share information
Award recognition
Provide visibility
Enhance reputation
Ensure belonging
Provide contacts
Demonstrate Understanding
Vote acceptance
Give backing
Show gratitude

Spread esteem
Offer comfort
Adapted from A.R. Cohen and D.L. Bradford, *Influence without Authority* (Wiley, 1990)

Take the often vexed question of the allocation of resources in an organisation. Much private angst – and open anger – is caused in inter-departmental conflicts by the suspicion of being 'nobbled' in a budget war.

ACTIVITY 54

Have you ever been disappointed by an inadequate award in a budgetary exercise? Were you aware that somebody else did much better than you for no apparent business reason?

Of course, there is stiff competition for resources in any organisation and it is easy to become overly partisan when fighting for resources for your own group. Where there are winners there are losers, and not all losers accept their fate with equanimity.

Supporting others to succeed in obtaining, maintaining and retaining the resources they want to accomplish their work tasks, when otherwise they might become losers, is a powerful influencing currency – when used with discrimination.

ACTIVITY 55

Look around your organisation and identify who is actively seeking funding for a project. In theory, how could you support their efforts? (Ignore your own interests for this exercise.)

Supporting everybody debases support as a currency; rationing it increases its scarcity value.

Blinkered self-promotion at the expense of others is risky because it creates multiple enemies among the losers, and among those who fear the outcome when they join a resource queue with you in it.

A reputation for getting what you want raises your profile as a powerful player. But a demonstrable reputation for being powerful enough to help (selected) others get what they want raises your reputation for influence even more.

ACTIVITY 56

Recollect incidents in which you have helped others to get the decisions they wanted by your interventions. What effects did this have on your relationships with them?

Favours done are favours owed and those in search of your favours will make tracks to your door. (Beware, though, of those who seek to curry favour with you, using flattery and ingratiation – you'll only get back the same worthless currency they try to sell you.)

Where you cannot help managers to get the resources they believe they require, it is better to remain neutral. If you cannot exchange the currencies of support, you can avoid exchanging the negative currencies of obstruction. ('If you can't help, don't hinder.')

LIGHT ON A PROBLEM

Amazingly, in the famous Hawthorn experiments at the Western Electric Factory (1924-32) conducted by Elton Mayo of Harvard Business School, when the researchers improved the workroom lighting, productivity improved and then when they made it worse, it continued to improve! Apparently, being the focus of attention was a significant influence on the behaviour of the employees participating in the experiments.

People like to be noticed.

Smarmy recognition speeches are obligatory for winners of

Oscars and recognition is also valued by many who deserve, or believe they deserve, public acknowledgement for their contributions. Not acknowledging somebody when there is good reason to do so, and when you have the opportunity, causes deep offence. Deliberately and publicly acknowledging a rival's contribution, especially a deadly rival, does wonders for your reputation as a fair-minded peacemaker and confuses your rival.

Recognition as an influencing currency is closely related to visibility. Some people like visibility; a few can never get enough of it.

Most politicians and some chief executives crave visibility and it is a sure sign of the visibility currency at work when a senior manager allows her organisation's press pack to carry multiple photographs of her.

If you can supply someone you want to influence with visibility, you won't do yourself much good by deliberately withholding it. Visibility is evidence of recognition. When you share visibility with others – especially to the point of self-denying self-effacement in their favour – you pile up credits in the influencing bank faster than most alternatives, assuming, of course, that the target manager prefers to trade in visibility. In contrast, self-promotion at another's expense is destructive of influence and encourages *sotto voce* mockery by one's peers.

Most people trade in anything that enhances their positive reputation, however they measure it. Undermining reputations by gossip, rumour and innuendo is a certain way to undermine your influence. If it is too embarrassing to defend someone's reputation, try silence.

Influence by building positive relationships with many people in lots of places in and around the organisation. Understanding what they are about – their intentions and aspirations, and their difficulties and challenges – as you must, is best accomplished as you grow relationships with them. This, necessarily, is a slow process.

Not threatening the present positions of other people, both

when it fits your goals and when it does not, is important when they feel insecure or are known to be vulnerable. Trading in threats to their position undermines your relationship with them. Being overly keen to replace them – 'carrying their coffins on your back' – is not productive with them or with onlookers.

Trading in backing people is better than back-stabbing them.

Ultimately, relationships are up close and personal. Expressing private gratitude for things they do for you is not just good manners, for example. Gratitude is all too easily forgotten, yet it takes only moments to transact and has an effect disproportionate to the effort involved.

ACTIVITY 57

In which currencies do you wish to transact? Make a list from those in Figure 13.1 and add any others not mentioned.

The knack of using influencing currencies is to identify which currencies are sought by which individuals and then deliver them. Your influence on potential allies is likely to be greater when they perceive that you consistently supply the currencies they seek.

In short, your allies (not you) perceive that you serve their interests. Of course, doing the opposite – damaging their sense of well-being or frustrating their interests – ultimately eliminates your influence.

Not everybody seeks to transact in any old influencing currency, nor will any particular person accept 'payment' in a specific currency from anybody offering it. People don't and won't. They are often as fussy over currencies as they are about those with whom they transact. Also, they are irritated by people who 'misread' their preferred currencies, such as when you hold back information (a powerful currency) they need to do their job or to pursue their own influencing projects.

Remember, Figure 13.1 is a selected list of labels for some commonly preferred currencies and not a scientifically defined taxonomy. One person's sense of inspiration, for example, may differ markedly from another's. You had better know the difference and identify the version that satisfies that particular recipient.

To influence people who deal in inspirational currencies, like vision, excellence and ethical principles, you are more likely to succeed if you demonstrate that you share their version of their vision.

PAS HAVE MOUTHS AS WELL AS EARS

At a project planning meeting, a manager criticised the CEO's obsession with her 'vision' for the company and mocked the time they had 'wasted' recently in (dis)agreeing on the latest 'mission statement'.

His views were not incorrect so much as injudicious.

The CEO's personal assistant was at the meeting. She mildly rebutted a factual inaccuracy he made but otherwise said nothing. Far from backing off, the manager continued expressing his trenchant views on CEO's sense of priorities throughout the rest of the meeting. No doubt the PA reported her version of his remarks to the CEO.

What did he gain by his impatient and intemperate tirade? Less than 'not much'. He was sidelined for a few months and left in high dudgeon because the CEO would not fund his project plans.

Leaders identify their role closely with their vision. They are irritated by scepticism, pessimism, conflicting visions and criticism. They cannot abide the people whom they perceive as obstacles to the achievement of their vision. They prefer people who solve problems with solutions consistent with the leader's vision. To influence leaders you must be seen to help and not hinder – you must be part of the solution and not part of the problem.

The same goes for the inspirational currency of 'excellence'. If the targets of your influence proselytise for excellence in everything they do, a reputation for sloppy work, or a tolerance of it, is a burden not an aid to your influence. But it goes further than that.

People who trade in the currency of excellence (however they define it) demand that you support their ethos on all occasions. That means that you avoid any hint of mocking, undermining or criticising what for them is a crusade. And you had better tolerate only excellent standards in your own work (a 'safe pair of hands').

Always remember your vulnerability to gossip about what you say to people in 'private' and the near certainty of its getting back to rival bidders for influence.

As for influencing people imbued with a sense that everything they do is strong on ethical principles, it is not helpful to become known for short-cuts, manoeuvres and an absence of ethical principles. It is best to treat what the ethically imbued profess at face value. If you suspect humbug in a person's flaunting of his or her ethics, it is best not to share your suspicions, or to comfort those who reveal similar suspicions. Influencers keep their own counsel.

Organisations are task oriented. This creates opportunities to influence the people charged with accomplishing the tasks (and to undermine your influence by failing to facilitate their efforts).

ACTIVITY 58

Conduct a quick assessment of your relationships with the people around you in your organisation.

The task may be simple (checking a form and passing it on) or complex (assembling many components into a circuit board) and people striving to complete their tasks are influenced by those who make them easier than by those who add to their difficulties (real or imagined).

ANSWERS TO SELF-ASSESSMENT TEST 13

1. (a) More than likely this is what she is after because raising her living standards is in her interests and with more money spent on education a pay rise is an almost inevitable outcome.

   (b) Possibly she is worried about the education of young children and in so far as she is a teacher, she has an interest in this activity attracting more resources. As salaries account for up to 80 per cent of the educational budget, teachers tend to gain personally from more spending on education.

   (c) Could be, but whether this is driven by a willingness to reduce the proportion of the education budget spent on teachers' salaries and raise the proportion spent on educational tools (books, computers, and suchlike) is not obvious.

2. (a) Probably, but brilliant surgeons are pig ignorant of anything outside their field.

   (b) Most certainly not. Surgeons are at the top of the income range in a hospital and soon let you know if their high earnings and other privileges are threatened.

SELF-ASSESSMENT TEST 14

1. You are attempting to persuade the CEO that the company should back your proposal for a dot.com development in the retail division. The technical director outlines to the CEO the investment required for on-line servers and POP access to facilitate customers buying on a secure line. She surprises you by commenting that she has reservations about the business case, which is not within her remit. Is this:
   (a) an example of her usual reputation for being a loose cannon?
   (b) an example of her disloyalty to the team?
   (c) an example of a gap in your preparations for the meeting?

2. Managing in a competitive economy you should be aware:
   (a) of everything the competition does?
   (b) of anything the competition does that affects you?
   (c) of some of the things the competition does?

3. Your project got trashed by the senior managers. Partly, this was because some of your team did not support it publicly and two criticised it at the crucial meeting. Another factor was the surprise appearance of a rival proposal that appeared to be less risky. You believe such a proposal is a waste of money and a waste of the great opportunity which your project addressed. Do you:
   (a) make your views known on the rival proposal?
   (b) berate the team members who criticised it and castigate those who did not support it?
   (c) review how you conducted your influencing effort in support of your project?

CHAPTER 14

Tangled webs, myopic worriers and bumpy rides

or how to survive with allies like these

Cedric is bright. I mean bright. If there was a Nobel prize for controlling human brain waves Cedric would win it. Maybe if Einstein was still alive it would be a close-run contest, but nowadays Cedric would walk it.

That's the problem. Cedric is so bright he's lost the plot, or more accurately he never found it. Give Cedric a technical problem and he goes straight to the solution. He can see solutions while most of his colleagues are still chewing over the details, trying to get a fix on a solution that holds up for more than a few minutes. By then, Cedric has delivered his solution and is waiting for his colleagues to catch up.

There is no dissembling with Cedric. He goes straight to the point. He doesn't hold back anything. If the project is a non-runner he says so, without any attempt to spare the project sponsor's feelings. A flaw is a flaw. A non-runner is a non-runner. Why waste time on it? So he doesn't. If his colleagues continue discussing it, he switches off and fiddles with his lap-top. He leaves the meeting if they discuss the non-runner for more than ten minutes, and pops back every now and again to re-join if the subject has changed.

He is saved by his technical brilliance. The company needs him because it needs the technical expertise Cedric and his team provide. He also puts in long hours, which often counts in busy enterprises.

What Cedric lacks is commercial acumen. That is bad enough in a commercial business. He also lacks a sensitivity to the requirements of people politics. That is a burden in any organisation. He always speaks his mind and gives unvarnished answers to any questions.

Now, it is not that his colleagues wish him to deliberately lie but they would all like him to know when to say something and when to shut up.

For example, if Cedric speaks on a subject upon which he has a technical opinion, he may very well add that he does not think the project should go forward. This is disconcerting to his colleagues who have invested vast amounts of political capital in getting partner departments to agree to the project as it stands. With departments that have varying degrees of enthusiasm for the project anyway, such remarks from Cedric are music to their ears. They cash in their chips and quit the game, citing Cedric's opinions as the reason, even though his opinions on the business aspects of the project have no merit.

Naturally, this drives Cedric's colleagues into despair, especially when the audience to which he reveals his reservations are investors, venture capitalists or fund managers. He also did it several times while his own Chief Executive Officer was evaluating reports from his colleagues on a major project upon which they had spent thousands of hours preparing. Cedric's justification for his frankness was based upon his belief that with another five million dollars investment, and critically, another 10 months beyond an already delayed alpha test, his team could produce a 'much better product worth doing'.

In short, Cedric is a loose cannon. His undoubted technical competence gives him an unwarranted authority in business decisions, about which he has no competence.

ACTIVITY 59

Do you have or know of a Cedric in your organisation? How would you deal with him (or her)?

Cedric's business colleagues have confronted him about his behaviour. These confrontations tend to be tense. Cedric stoutly defends himself by saying he 'never knowingly lies' about his opinions when asked for them and he will not be induced to 'lie by omission'. Cedric sees preparations for a meeting with the CEO or investors as the weaving of tangled webs of deceit unless he speaks up and tells (his version of) the truth. Against such near saintly conviction his business colleagues wring their hands in despair.

ACTIVITY 60

To what extent would you agree with Cedric about the duty to be absolutely honest in your opinions in fields in which you have no competence?

One of the problems with academically bright people is that they can be amazingly dim when it comes to business acumen. I once remarked boldly to an audience of senior academics that having heard their views on fees, it was a 'good job there were no intelligence tests before people were appointed as professors'. (The outcome is clear evidence that giving others the benefit of one's opinions is a no-no for influencers, especially those seeking promotion!)

The Cedrics of this world are an absolute menace when it comes to strategy. They are the closest you will get to myopic visionaries. Because they are eyes-down-focused they cannot help but be disruptive in their contributions to strategy discussions. On the technical discussions they are fine but on the business decisions they are, er, adrift.

When Cedrics are joined by what Lord Nelson called 'the children of war', you are in for a bumpy ride – and this is before you get to market. Remember, these guys are on your team, not the competition's.

Now Lord Nelson was not being personal when he logged his comment. He was describing a phenomenon known long before the Battle of Copenhagen in 1801 (Julius Caesar said something similar two thousand years before) and it has been experienced many times since. Whenever managers discuss 'the competition', the voices of the children of war are raised.

Nelson wrote that the Danish defences 'only look formidable to those who are children of war'. And they certainly did. Armed floating hulks, heavily armed stone-walled forts, floating batteries and armed warships against ten of Nelson's ships, which were anchored in a narrow channel, with sand banks behind them and no room to pass. Where they anchored was where they would slug it out, literally to the death. Copenhagen was the most bloody of all naval battles experienced by the Royal Navy.

Chris is very good at what she does. Her senior position requires her to contribute to overall strategy decisions and she also speaks regularly with almost everybody in the organisation. She is one of Nelson's children of war. Influencers need her on-side because what she says affects (and sometimes infects) others.

The competition always looks fearsome. This is not to say that the competition is a great big cuddly pussy cat that rolls over and likes its tummy tickled. Of course not. Competition is a serious business, best not tackled by children. But competition is not an invincible, all-conquering, no prisoners taken affair. There is no need to panic just because it looks formidable.

Chris always worries about the competition. If she spots any evidence of a competitive marketing campaign, she draws everybody's attention to it, sometimes copying their advertisements for circulation. If the competition advertises in the tiny Auchtermuchty Gazette, then she wants a salvo placed in response. She wants adverts in the most expensive business press, either before the competition places theirs or because the competition was in there with full-colour folded-page pull-outs last week. If her boss asked her for rate cards for television advertising, complete with jingles, I bet she has the details in her files already.

ACTIVITY 61

How fierce do you believe the competition is in your line of work? On what is this belief based? How much has your market share changed in the past five years?

If total sales is your criterion for success, then the slightest drop causes concern. If profit is more important, a drop in total sales may not be of much concern and could be a cause for celebration if profits rose as a result. If you are heading an influencing effort to change the strategic focus from sales to profit you do not welcome interventions by Chris warning of impending doom from falling total sales as she reads the monthly sales figures (her department compiles them).

It's no good berating Chris for her myopia. You had better get her on-side. And quickly. You had better share your vision of a profitable strategy and convince her of its soundness. Hammering her down works, but only until you are out of her sight. She will attack the flaw in your strategy (sales are falling!) to all and sundry and some key players who will spread her doubts too. If she can throw in some of the astonishing details she happens to have found of a competitor's marketing campaign, you could be in for a rough time. Feelings of doom precede those of panic.

The road to influence can become a bumpy ride. Roughly, this means you will not get it all your own way. People have doubts, which they share, quietly. They mull over what you say (and if you say but a little of what you are about, it does not take overly long for them to mull). They are influenced by people around them and by passing perceptions of events.

They may have a 'theory', which they have nursed for many years, about how their world works and which are the decisive forces in it. For example, 'in this business it's all down to price'; 'we are a people business'; 'our customers want no compromise on quality'; 'in retail its location, location, location' and so on. Your vision may not fit their theory. So you are wrong, bad for them and bad for the organisation.

ACTIVITY 62

Do you have a theory of the decisive forces that operate in your business or organisation? Could you summarise it in a few words?

Bumpy rides come in many forms. Outright opposition at meetings is one form but by far not the most insidious. Though outright opposition causes problems and requires energy and political capital to fight, and exposes you to risk of non-performance against the critics, it is of a different order to the silent, guerrilla warfare conducted by the unconvinced, and usually uninformed, critics who undermine your vision from a multitude of positions. Some say you are empire building, too ambitious and too much of a risk-taker. Others say your plans are flawed, not properly researched and poorly conceived.

As the critics influence the persons upon whom you rely to implement the vision, they can do far more damage than open critics who make rallies against you at management meetings. Given that your vision competes with other people's visions, you may expect fissures in the unanimity of support which you hope will be behind you and your project.

Having Cedric and Chris in your team is a burden and it is too easy for you to become diverted into waging war on them. You certainly cannot ignore them but you as certainly must not make them targets for your wrath. If they are not on board you have some convincing to do to bring them on board. They represent different problems for you. Cedric types have specialist blinkers on and an overblown fear of business morality; Chris types are overly impressed by their fears of competition, or whatever theories they have about your business.

Nobody is asking Cedric to lie. A project based on lies and deceit would not survive the bumpy ride it will get anyway. Cedric, however, is expected to exercise discretion. He should raise his doubts in team meetings and not rehearse them in front of the CEO. His doubts must be answered at the team meetings and worked through until either he or you is convinced by the other. Time properly spent in serious discussion legitimises self-discipline later.

Nobody denies that Chris should be aware of the threat of competition. However, competition can be exaggerated. The market for products and ideas is competitive. That is what gives capitalism and democracy great strength over rivals. But only paranoid dictators fear the tiniest voice of dissent. That's why they jail poets and hang authors. Only paranoid managers fear the rival's adverts and want to spend vast sums fighting ghosts.

That other teams compete for the attention of the CEO is something to celebrate, not condemn. That other firms fight for the attention of your customers is not something to worry obsessively about. You have to make sure that what you offer is of better value. If you do this then your influencing project inside the organisation need fear no rival.

ANSWERS TO SELF-ASSESSMENT TEST 14

1. (a) It may be an example of her reputation but this is not as important as (c).
   (b) She may have been disloyal but this is not as important as (c).
   (c) Absolutely. You have not prepared properly. Knowing of her reputation you did nothing to ensure she did not become a loose cannon.

2. (a) You should be concentrating on everything that you do and not everything rivals are doing.
   (b) To select anything they do that affects would require you to survey everything they do in case it affects you, which is not much different from (a).
   (c) Yes. Be aware without becoming obsessed.

3. (a) Unlikely to be helpful, no matter how you feel. If you are right the rivals will demonstrate this for you. If you are

wrong, they will be twice as serious as rivals.

(b) No doubt the normal response but not as important to you as (c).

(c) Yes. And see Chapters 15 and 16 for details of FAME.

SELF-ASSESSMENT TEST 15

1. You attend an inter-departmental meeting with a 10-item agenda, which will probably last most of the morning. You have views on eight of the items because they relate to aspects of your department's activities. On how many of the items on the agenda will you contribute your views?
   (a) eight?
   (b) ten?
   (c) none?

2. Your allies at work are:
   (a) your friends?
   (b) anybody with whom you are friendly?
   (c) anybody with whom you have common and supportive informal goals?

3. Which has the greatest impact on an outcome you seek in an influencing project:
   (a) the people for and against the outcome?
   (b) unexpected events?
   (c) the arguments put up by both sides for and against the outcome?

CHAPTER 15

Playing FAME
or Sam's road to influence

Sam, an ambitious politician, worked her way through the lower ranks of a new parliamentary intake. In one evening she gave me a Master Class in influence, for which I am, of course, eternally grateful.

Now, Sam (known as Samantha to her parents) might be embarrassed to see her ideas in print (though knowing her, she might also be secretly pleased – and she'll soon let me know if she isn't).

I must have caught her on a good day – or rather evening – when we accidentally met again after many years. We last saw each other as students, though I had, of course, seen her many times since on television.

She was remarkably frank about her professional work and she had obviously put a lot of effort into her career in mainstream politics, not just because she is female (which, until recently, was a severe handicap for those with parliamentary ambitions) but also because her chosen party was not popular. She won her seat in a by-election and kept it in the General Election.

Over several hours – and much Chianti – we talked about the different paths our lives had taken (with mutual 'if only?' musing). While our nostalgic projections were all very interesting, with their hints of regret, I kept my composure by focusing on the fascinating operational, as opposed to party political, side of Sam's career.

What follows is a summary of Sam's seminar. Her insights were stunning, so much so that I made detailed notes of them on the night sleeper train to Edinburgh. I also featured something resembling Sam's system in a workshop for a dozen Euro-PR functionaries a week later. I don't recollect what the PR people thought of my version of this system, but I do know it scores highly in post-workshop debriefings. Let's see what you think – but only if you agree to make your judgements only *after* you try Sam's system out.

Sam was adamant that walking into meetings and relying on reacting immediately to events as they unfold is a prelude to obscurity. 'You either open your mouth when you should keep it shut, or you lose your nerve when you should open it,' she insisted. (She also said, 'If you waited for men to pause and let you speak, you'd wait until they thought it was time for you to make the tea.')

Her substantive point was valid. You are always at a disadvantage if others have prepared what they want to say and do and you haven't. Lack of pre-meeting preparation only makes life more difficult for yourself.

ACTIVITY 63

Recall the circumstances of any meeting in which you suspected that some people had co-ordinated their contributions in advance.

Sam advised that aspirants (a word she used as if it was in danger of eradication from the dictionary) must read the minutes, check the agenda and decide beforehand on what topics they intend to contribute. At the meeting Sam would never have to read Chapter 1! Talking on everything is a classic beginner's mistake – or, as my grandma often put it, 'Empty vessels make the most sound.'

ACTIVITY 64

Check the agenda for an upcoming meeting and note how many

items you could speak to and compare with those upon which you have nothing to contribute. Is there more of the former than the latter?

I know, preparation takes time and you're busy (ain't we all?) but it is time well spent. True, preparation alone does not guarantee success – you still have to execute your influencing strategy – but preparation significantly simplifies the process.

Sam mentioned some simple 'things' she always does in preparation. The main claim she made for her system was that it works and, after some years of applying her system, I concur. I have no idea, and didn't question, why she calls them 'things'. I didn't want to interrupt her flow, nor to give any hint that I thought she was wittering on. I had no idea when she might make her excuses and leave. Since we had sat down in the restaurant, she had repeatedly warned me that she might 'have to dash away at any moment to vote' – and I didn't think she was trying to impress me.

Sam made no claim that the 'things' she did were scientific. She began applying them arbitrarily and could not remember where they originated. She said she picked them up as she went along by taking tips from people whose advice worked. As she elaborated on her system, it seemed to me to be no more than mental back-of-an-envelope doodles. But let's follow Sam's system and see if they might work for you.

First, let me replace the ponderous title, 'influencing project', with the anything but frivolous word, *FAME*, and let's define FAME as a distinct self-contained sequence of actions for a purpose. Sam, I should add, is in no way responsible for this acronym. Aspirants, as Sam calls them, incorrigibly find it easier to remember a mnemonic than they do otherwise.

FAME is my mnemonic for Sam's system:

Focus
Access
Mobilise
Execute

FOCUS

Influencing, Sam insisted, requires focus. Influence is undertaken for a purpose. Aimless influencing is as pointless as its cousin, aimless discontent, and as unsatisfying. Influencing is more than having friendly relations. In FAME you have a serious purpose in mind.

So, the aspirant must decide for what purpose she wants influence. What do you intend to achieve? Or putting it another way, I offered, quoting the Labour politician, Aneurin Bevan: 'The burdens of public office are too onerous to serve for trivial ends.' Sam snorted (either it was the wrong politician, or I had stolen her punch line).

Objectives, she continued, dictate the policies you pursue but events (I refrained from offering Macmillan on events) and new information change your policies. Flexibility is required because, while your objectives may endure, the means to achieve them and the obstacles in their way dictate tactical changes. Larger stakes, of course, are different from smaller stakes, but the methods used to influence for any stakes are not all that different. The systems you use are the same or similar; only your ends are different.

Focusing is best dealt with in layers, beginning with a 'top-level' objective, say, 'to be appointed head of the department by December'. Objectives, remember, should always be SMART (Specific, Measurable, Achievable, Realistic, and Time bound).

To achieve a top-level objective, we derive several lower-level objectives, intermediate in scope, such as 'expand my departmental functions horizontally and vertically', or 'increase my departmental presence on two key investment committees', and suchlike. Achieving your lower-level objectives will deliver your top-level objective (you hope).

But Sam's main point about focusing on a clear (SMART) purpose to guide your activity is surely uncontroversial?

ACCESS

Sam insisted that you must identify the people who may be important to your objectives. You cannot do much except with and through people. Misanthropy is not an option (and for Sam, of course, misogyny was out of the question).

She also kept referring to her colleagues as 'actors' and on the train home this rankled. I prefer to think of the people we work with in FAME as 'players'.

Shakespeare's distinction between 'acting' and 'playing' is pertinent (*As You Like It*):

> *All the world's a stage.*
> *And all the men and women merely players:*
> *They have their exits and their entrances;*
> *And one man in his time plays many parts . . . '*

Actors adopt fictitious roles written by others and when the curtain falls, return to the grim realities of their lives. Players are real people, who in their lifetimes never cease to play their parts. They cry real tears, feel real pain, shed real blood, laugh real laughs, and suffer and enjoy real emotions. Players are real; actors merely act.

Having met many of Sam's fellow politicians over the years, though, I can understand why the word 'actor' springs to her mind. Some of them deserve Oscars for their performances.

For each phase of FAME there are different players. Having identified the players in your FAME, evaluate your current state of access, or lack of access, to them. As you access the players – and you must access all of them – mentally tick off their names.

If you do not (yet) know their names, you must find out who they are from their department or organisation. Access, remember, is about making contact, not about making lists (GOYA!).

150

ACTIVITY 65

Think of a recent FAME project in which a number of people were players. Name them.

Most players in FAME may be 'strangers' to you. Some of them may already know each other and they may have independent connections of which you know nothing. It is also worthwhile remembering that players to whom you deliver 'special' messages, *entre nous*, might compare notes with the other people they know.

Influencers who speak with 'forked tongues' are easily spotted (and as swiftly rejected).

In FAME you have access to players who are your colleagues and it is unforgivable if you do not know them (take three showers immediately!). Knowing the players has advantages, except when they know you for the wrong reasons. However, you must contact them (GOYA or GOTT). And you still have to access those you do not yet know.

Not accessing as yet unknown players at the first opportunity is as close to wilful negligence as an influencer can get. It raises questions about your seriousness. In politics, and in organisations, many aspirants fall off the 'greasy pole' without a shove from a rival – they jump of their own volition.

ACTIVITY 66

Think of someone whom you could call right now to report some useful (for them) information, or whose support in some matter you would be happy to enlist. GOYA or GOTT, or as Jerry Rubin, the 1960s student radical, enjoined us: do it!

MOBILISE

The way Sam described mobilising her allies made eminent sense. In all worthwhile contests of ideas, she said, with the conviction of somebody who needs no reassurance, there are 'those for you, those against and those who profess to be neutral'.

Sam insisted that it was important to name the players who were for or against you. I slightly shifted her distinction beyond this. I suggest you also assess how important these people are *relative to each other*. In other words, conceive of the people 'for and against' you as being forces, some stronger than others, pushing against each other. At any one moment there are forces pushing for positive changes in the status quo and some pushing against disruptions to the status quo. The status quo prevails to the extent that the forces pushing for the change are cancelled out, or overwhelmed, by the forces pushing against the change.

Politicians, except extremists and obsessive single issue fanatics, seldom permanently push for changes to the status quo. Certainly, Sam wasn't – she had one eye on the Whips' office and another on the serried ranks of party activists (a difficult bunch to please in any political party). Likewise, on some occasions you may act like the famous *sans-culottes* of revolutionary France in 1789 and on other occasions like a reactionary *Junker* from Berlin in 1889 (if you are permanently one or the other, you have no influence and are reading this book as penance for a wasted life).

ACTIVITY 67

Think of the competing solutions to a current problem at work. To what extent can you identify the people who favour, and those who oppose, these solutions?

Clearly, to change a situation, the forces for change must over-come the forces against. If you want to change a situation, you work to strengthen the forces for change and simultaneously weaken the forces against. Meanwhile, players against the change will work to weaken the forces for change and strengthen the forces against.

Sam graphically illustrated her assessment of the politics of change with 'insider' accounts of current conflicts within her party's leadership. A tabloid journo hearing her anecdotes (which I could never reveal, of course) would have thought he had died and gone to heaven.

Some forces, because of their impact are more important than others. Highly important forces attract the most attention (assuming they can be strengthened or weakened), although a typical error, Sam reminded me, is to focus mainly on the easily influenced forces, irrespective of their impact. For example, you spend more time influencing people already on your side – 'preaching to the converted' – and you avoid more difficult targets entrenched against you, or difficult to get at (shades of a poor GOYA!). You seldom find Sam at the her party's conference fringe meetings of the tendency she supports, because she spends as much time as she can with party members with whom she disagrees.

You might do similarly by avoiding the exclusive tea-break and lunchtime cliques of the likeminded. It is better to be inclusive than exclusive, Sam said.

Judgement is called for, not only to discriminate by the degree of importance of the forces to the outcome, but also to discriminate in favour of the susceptibility of a force to your influence. Again, it is best to keep your strategies simple. While you assess the degrees of importance of individuals as low, medium or high, you grade their relative susceptibility to your influence as 'easy', 'moderate' or 'difficult'.

ACTIVITY 68

How would you grade the importance of some of the players in a current problem? Who is the easiest to influence, who moderately difficult and who the most difficult? (And with which group do you spend most of your time?)

Influencing works through people. Your allies are those who mobilise on your behalf. All others are potential allies – or rabid opponents. But supping with strange bedfellows, so to speak, is more common than you would think. In this respect, Sam's idea of a contest between the forces is helpful. Label the forces with the names of people you know to be (or likely to be) favourable or unfavourable to your project.

You may not know the names of some players, suggesting that you do not know where they stand and that you have more work to do (so GOYA and GOTT!).

You have a great deal more to do besides identifying players for and against your objectives. You have to take account of the arguments people could use, for and against the issues (by 'argument' I do not refer to a rowdy altercation but to an influencing argument conducted without rancour). Also, you must be wary of any relevant events that have a bearing on the outcome you seek.

Sam's insight into competing forces enhances the quality of your information because it focuses on what has to be done to secure the desired outcome. Identify allies and potential allies and suggest lines of approach to weaken opposition and to strengthen your support.

Experience suggests that it is often easier to weaken an opponent's pressure than it is to strengthen your own. Be careful because it is always easier, I suggest, to be destructive than creative. Overdosing on destructive argument destroys your sense of balance and is fed by bitterly contested argument from those you are up against. You do not want to appear overly negative when attempting to weaken an opponent's pressure and you must curb your frustration when tempted to personalise disputes.

EXECUTE

Sam insisted that there are two parts to execution. The first is to be clear on what it is that you want to happen (and why), and the second is to have clear ideas about who is to do what, by when and with whom on your behalf.

Given your objectives, and in the light of your subsequent contacts with the players, what specifically do you want to happen? Has anything emerged from your contacts with these players to modify your original objectives?

A review of your objectives requires attention to detail. It may require a revision of your objectives, or the generation of new initiatives, with some initiatives scheduled to happen in sequence, others in parallel. Influencers work to multiple agendas and must keep track of many moving targets.

Sam uses realistic strategies to strengthen the forces for and weaken the forces against her objectives ('You seldom get your own way totally, and trying to achieve fantasy "wish lists" mostly ensures disappointment,' she said).

The realism of your influencing objectives is tested when you detail to your allies individual tasks, responsibilities and behaviours to be accomplished within agreed time scales. Unrealistic objectives soon reveal themselves when partial outcomes from contacts with the players fall far short of your objectives. If the objectives are realistic and still you fall short of your objectives, then your allies are unreliable – a not uncommon occurrence, I might add.

For example, your FAME requires a departmental head to support your stance by the end of the month (a good SMART objective) but, while broadly sympathetic – at least he listens to your pitch – he is sceptical of the radical steps you propose. He makes uncertain commitments, he qualifies his statements with excuses, he is vague on taking matters further and he generally acts as if he has other things on his mind. Above all, he becomes difficult to contact.

Clearly, he does not share your sense of urgency and certainly not your commitment.

ACTIVITY 69

Have you experience of an ally fudging her support for something to which you feel strongly committed? Have you ever been put in the same position in respect of something upon which another person is more keen than you?

If you have not moved forward with your allies within your timetable, you are not going to execute your influence programme timeously and, if your timetable drifts, so will your objectives. On the other hand, realistic objectives executed by reliable allies sustain their own momentum.

The execution of your FAME is a combination (for and against) of the players, arguments and events. Over none of these forces do you have total control. You only have the opportunity to exert influence on them, or to cope with their influence on you.

How players are disposed towards your objectives is down to their perceptions. What are the relative strengths of the arguments for or against your objectives?

To do justice to your assessment of other people's perceptions you must become aware of the arguments against your case and not just with its merits. To influence the case against you, you need more than a rehearsal of the arguments supporting your views, and probably more than an attack on the people opposing you.

Ignoring the possibility of unexpected events in FAME is serious folly – the more so when events intrude on your 'best laid schemes'. Events severely test the depth of your support (a drugs bust), your morale (an endless press barrage) and your energy (a pregnancy). Fortunately, most events come with the territory and you are expected to cope without collapsing into crises.

Sam recounted some of the unexpected events in her career and how she (only just) coped. 'Overcoming events toughens you,' said Sam, 'but letting them overcome you, toughens your opponents.' This struck me later as the hardened wisdom of an altogether different woman to the one I thought I knew so well at university.

ANSWERS TO SELF-ASSESSMENT TEST 15

1. (a) Not unless you have something pertinent to say on all eight of them. You have views on lots of subjects but it is

not imperative that you speak about them at all management meetings.

(b) Certainly not. If this is happens, you talk too much to be effective.

(c) Maybe a bit extreme if some of the items are really important to you and you have prepared for them. But saying nothing is not a bad practice to try every now and again.

2. (a) Some of them might be, but being friends is not sufficient to make them allies.

(b) You should be friendly towards lots of people – there is no point stirring up animosity for the sake of it – always remember that some of these people will be friendly towards some other people who may not be on your side at all.

(c) Yes. Supporting each other and sharing a common goal are defining characteristics of allies.

3. (a) In FAME, the people have the most important impact. But not always. Usually, people, events and arguments combine to decide the outcome.

(b) In FAME, unexpected events have the most important impact. Again, not always.

(c) In FAME, the arguments put up for and against have the most important impact. But not always. As (a) above.

SELF-ASSESSMENT TEST 16

1. In FAME the players divide into strong supporters, strong opponents and lukewarm supporters, opponents and neutrals. Which group is most significant for FAME?
   (a) lukewarm and neutral?
   (b) strong opponents?
   (c) strong supporters?

2. You totally oppose an initiative pushed by a colleague and must stop it at all costs (for whatever reason). Do you:
   (a) fight at every opportunity for a total rejection on grounds that the initiative has no merits?
   (b) fight at selected opportunities for a total rejection on grounds that the initiative has few merits?
   (c) fight at every opportunity for a partial acceptance on grounds that the initiative may have merits but further studies are required to establish their nature, extent and consequences?

3. Sixty-eight per cent of your colleagues do not support your initiative according to a 'For' or 'Against' survey carried out by the boss. Do you:
   (a) accept the verdict and withdraw your initiative?
   (b) sample the people who voted against to see how intensely they opposed your initiative?
   (c) carry on regardless of the boss's poll?

CHAPTER 16

Playing FAME in your world

or nuances are not for nothing

Since my meeting with Sam – an unexpected and pleasant event – I have encouraged many mangers to play FAME. The FAME most managers play in their organisations is different in context to Sam's, though no less serious.

After all, Sam's private seminar was from an accomplished professional politician playing FAME in a context a long way from yours and mine on at least two counts: one, her competitors are openly ambitious, adept, and goal driven to a much higher and near universal degree than ours, and two, they play FAME in the goldfish bowl of media and public scrutiny.

You, on the contrary, may be the only person playing FAME (or its equivalent) and you shun publicity. Politicians have inbuilt radar to spot a rival's moves and manoeuvres at long distance and what they do not detect, the half-dozen newspapers they scour a day report. They are obsessed by what their rivals say or do (and their rivals are not necessarily in a different party).

To adapt FAME to suit your circumstances you must appreciate a few of the nuances that soon become apparent as you play through the phases.

<u>YOUR FAME</u>

The first nuance to understand is that FAME is seldom played in a rigid linear sequence from F through to E. Tidiness suggests linear movement from Focus to Access, through Mobilise and finally to Execute, but real life ain't that tidy. Sometimes FAME sequences in a tidy manner but more often it does not, and you won't FAME for long before you realise that the phases can sequence in any direction.

FAME also includes a myriad of changing detail. Keeping track of this is a heavy burden. To lessen the burden, keep it simple. If you let the detail become too complex, FAME takes too much time to execute and, inevitably, is abandoned (quite rightly) by busy managers. For example, failing to identify all the players reveals instantly that you have work to do – who and where are they? If you don't know, who does?

ACTIVITY 70

Who in your organisation appears to know everybody and is willing to share information with you and initiate introductions?

To access the missing players, you must meet allies who know them and can describe their attitudes and how best to make an approach. Introductions are worth their weight in gold if this averts ice-cold canvassing. In the absence of introductions you have to cold canvass, and even hardened sales people hate a cold canvass. At this point the lazy are easily discouraged and drop out, which is good news for those who GOYA and get on with it (GOWI?).

You can't ignore gaps in your knowledge of the players, though when to approach them is a judgement call. Leaving gaps in your necessary knowledge about players is risky. Avoid that risk with FAME.

Sam was right – some players unambiguously are on your side; others against. A few of the players, you will soon notice, deserve to be listed on both sides – they are against you in some respects and for you in others! This Janus-like phenomenon is not un-usual. It is not evidence of widespread two-faced behaviour –

though be wary: apparent smiling assent from some people is deceptive. Their facial muscles say one thing, their cheating hearts another.

ACTIVITY 71

Has anybody behaved in a two-faced way with you recently? When did it become obvious what they were up to? What did you feel about their behaviour?

It is not always clear where some players stand. Publicly, because of their position, past associations or prejudices, they support their department's views, but in private conversation with you they may aver to something different.

Others genuinely are on both sides of the argument. They support the principle but not the detail or the timing; they oppose the principle, but support something being done to address the problem. Work on their hesitations and bolster their sympathies!

Some players start off in opposition only to switch sides during the campaign (and others originally in your camp may move in the reverse direction). You cannot but take account of swaying loyalties and the intrusion of unforeseen events – such as a major ally becoming ill, being arrested on serious charges, or innocently resigning.

ACTIVITY 72

Have you experienced a sudden event that removed a key ally from the scene in the midst of an important game? How did you cope?

In FAME, something could happen to cause players to pause while the 'problem' is addressed. This may mean retreating from Execution to Focus and starting over. Or while mobilising, new players force you to return to Access. Indeed, it may be necessary to mobilise repeatedly during FAME before you can execute some of your moves.

If you know which phase you are in, you can switch back and forth as the need arises, and work in one phase with some players and in another phase with others. That is why some would-be players react and complain, 'It's all too complicated!' How complicated it gets is up to you – remember, keep it simple. But if you let FAME become 'too complicated', think how complicated it becomes without FAME! Lack of structure creates a fog of *ad hoc* activity, which buries you in it.

WILL IT PLAY?

It is easy to become obsessed and to dismiss the doubts of sceptics as myopic. It is also easy to be discouraged by a player's apathy. Neither reaction is helpful.

If your colleagues are slow to appreciate your insights, be cautious. You need allies. If your allies cannot be roused, it is unlikely that those less disposed to your initiative will rally round in hot pursuit of your solution.

Not all ideas deserve to survive exposure to the people likely to be affected by them. In the myriad informal discussions taking place in side-meetings, over coffee, at lunch breaks and while journeying to meetings, as many flashes of insight are articulated as there are problems. Some scepticism is expressed in jest – those present laugh a little – some in anger. Which is why most ideas perish shortly after birth. Sometimes an idea floats and is then forgotten, unless for at least one person it nags away at the back of the mind, until he or she asks: 'Why not?'

'Why not?' may be answered at the first mention of the idea: 'We tried that once and it failed miserably.' If you accept that block, it kills it for good. However, it may start you wondering whether the situations are strictly analogous.

ACTIVITY 73

Think of the last time you had or heard a solution to a work-related problem that was discounted by colleagues because it had been tried before and allegedly found to be wanting.

Of the vast informal flow of ideas and solutions (many of them plain silly or otherwise impractical) only a few survive to be taken seriously. Ideas that survive remain fragile because ideas and solutions to problems are not judged solely or passively on their merits.

Some people react negatively to ideas because they were 'not invented here' and what these people did not invent they are against. Moreover, if they are hostile to its inventor, they doubly oppose it on emotional grounds. They fear the originator will reap 'undeserved' credit or some other benefit coveted by themselves.

Try out your solutions with trustworthy allies first. If they respond positively – even offer supportive suggestions – enrol them to effect the change. Ask them whom else you should see. They might suggest useful contacts or, better still, sponsor introductions to players who influence outcomes.

Radical changes take detailed planning to iron out all the defects (and all plans begin with inbuilt defects because you cannot anticipate every contingency).

Do not just harvest support and abandon it. Allies provide useful feedback on the workability of what you propose. Tap into their expertise by keeping them fully informed of changes to the plan and carefully consider their comments, criticisms and suggestions. Your plan has to become their plan too, if you are to make progress.

WHOM TO ACCESS?

Not all titular heads have the most influence in their function. The second-in-command, for example, may exercise more influence by virtue of his boss's lethargy, impending retirement or newness, and the deputy's closer contacts within the organisation, or from some other circumstance not captured in a formal organisational chart.

ACTIVITY 74

Have you experienced a titular head who did not run the function? Do you know of other cases where assistants or deputies know more about what goes on than their boss?

POWERFUL TITLES DO NOT MEAN POWERFUL PEOPLE

People who control access to important and influential people exert influence belied by their formal rankings. The Chief of Staff, if she controls access to a US President, exercises greater power than the Vice-President or members of the Cabinet. So does the President's private secretary, if the appointments diary is controlled from her desk just outside the Oval Office.

When trying to change minds and arguments, consider the dynamics of how a group of any size divides for or against any proposition.

Take the case where about half the people affected by your proposition are in favour and half are against. Is this a deadlock? Not necessarily. A 50:50 split can be a misleading measure of your proposal's prospects. It all depends on the intensity with which people are for and against your proposal, and, even more crucially, how those intensities shift throughout your FAME campaign.

ACTIVITY 75

In your experience, have you found that people have varying degrees of support or hostility to almost any proposition?

Some people, say, are very strongly in favour of your change and others are very strongly against. These individuals might form very small minorities. True, they may be noisy in their support or opposition, and inclined to exaggeration when expressing their views. Most people, however, usually have less strong views for or against proposals, with a fair proportion of them benignly neutral.

You do not want to drive people into opposition, so the first rule is not to talk to, or about, the people in FAME as if they are your most militant opponents. You want to pull people into supporting you and not drive them more firmly into your opponent's camp.

ACTIVITY 76

Which arguments have the greatest effect on you: (a) those that cast doubts on whether the change would work or could be afforded; (b) those that incorporate an outright denunciation of the proposal and of the people supporting it?

RANT AND LOSE SUPPORT

During student elections a university allowed candidates to visit lecture rooms and, with the permission of the lecturer, address the assembled students for a few minutes. My first-year class at that time had 400 students and so was regularly visited.

At one election for student president, there were two candidates who spoke to the class. The first spoke for the allotted three minutes saying what he would do to improve their lot (the details are trivial – gone were the days when students ranted against their lecturers as 'imperialist running dogs'). His rival spent his time solely and emotionally attacking his rival's mendacity, deviousness and, amazingly, his record the previous year as the student 'dance convenor'! His rival obviously had a great future because he said nothing in response to this tirade.

Guess who lost the election a week later? Yes, the ranter. I don't know what happened to him, but I expect he went into politics.

This again underlines the need to take seriously the doubts, fears and concerns of people who do not support your proposal with the same enthusiasm as you and your allies.

WINNING ALLIES

You win allies by arguing convincingly for your proposal and by weakening arguments against it. You do not have to convert everybody into supporters (especially the most strongly opposed). You only have to marginalise the intractable by winning over their lukewarm allies.

And this is where mobilising your allies is so important. If you remain the lone fighter, you rely on destiny or the fates to win your case. It is much better if others – many others – make your case to those who doubt that your proposal is needed or practicable.

Consensus generates momentum. Those only marginally opposed are susceptible to regular expressions of support from those whom they respect. Lukewarm opponents are your key target group.

Would-be influencers often make the elementary mistake of concentrating their fire – and their bile – on prominent opponents. They should concentrate, instead, on the near neutrals. Mild expressions of opposition are not tantamount to treason!

Your allies are not immune to swinging away from support or occasional doubts. The remedy is to keep in constant contact with them. Provide them with regular and enthusiastic infusions of the arguments for your proposal, preferably delivered by other allies.

ACTIVITY 77

Think of a powerful argument that was made against a position you supported and the effect on your commitment of not hearing a persuasive counter-argument or rebuttal relatively quickly. Did you sustain your support for your position, modify it or change sides?

The battle for the 'hearts and minds' of those affected by the change and of those who make decisions to implement the change, is not well served by a 'fire and forget' approach. Unless you keep the momentum going by reinforcing your arguments for support, doubts grow, advocates waver and allies make excuses and cool their ardour.

The most commonly used and successful blocking strategy against a proposal is to slow down the commitment process among its supporters, and your own waverers, by calling for 'more studies', 'reassessments', 'pilot trials', 'surveys of practices elsewhere', 'consultations of all interested parties', 'invitations to prominent critics' to ensure 'balance', 'full and proper costing of the implications', 'temporary moratoriums' and other similar devices.

ACTIVITY 78

Have you participated in a blocking device? Have you suffered from one?

Procedural battles are not just a test of the arguments for the proposal – they also test the endurance of its proponents.

HEADS WE WIN, TAILS YOU LOSE

Companies experimenting with genetically modified (GM)

foods are under pressure from campaigns against their introduction. The argument is partly scientific but mostly emotional. 'Frankenstein foods' was a recent newspaper headline, along with alarmist fears of letting a 'genie out of the bottle'.

Two other prongs of attack are under way. The first is to stop all experiments by calling for a 'moratorium' for rolling periods of five years. If the moratorium is adopted, GM opponents ensure themselves at least five years of campaigning to rouse public opinion to force their government to change its mind should it decide to end the moratorium.

The second is to block the food companies from transferring their experiments from countries that adopt the moratorium to moratorium-free countries by legally requiring all food products to be labelled if they have GM food ingredients. Ostensibly, this is to allow consumers 'choice' in what they eat. But choice is restricted if 'fear, uncertainty and doubt' – the FUD factor – stalks the imagination of consumers.

Faced with commercial doubts – far more potent than public opinion – food companies are unlikely to undertake expensive experimentation. Either way, the anti-GM campaigners win.

Where the radicalism of the proposal inhibits its adoption by cautious decision-makers, a 'salami' strategy is viable. You expose them to demonstrations of the benefits of your proposal ('a slice at a time') by trials, pilot schemes, experimental projects and suchlike. You build the alliance necessary to gain approval for the full version of change – assuming that your proposal proves successful.

People who oppose something usually find fault with the details. The devil, it has been said, lies in the detail, and a dismissive lament along the lines of 'Great in theory, *but...*' has broken the momentum of many a proposal. Therefore, it is absolutely essential that you respond effectively (and politely) to all objections.

THEORY AND PRACTICE

A successful business owner was invited to address a seminar for final-year students. He recounted his experience in running a counter-trade operation in Africa. In the vote of thanks speech by the professor, he was told: 'Your experience may have worked in practice, but it would never work in theory!'

It is not prudent to dismiss the people who raise detailed objections (even if you feel you have excellent grounds for exposing their foibles). It is the effect on the neutral and lukewarm supporters and opponents influenced by the objection and not your assessment of the objection's (or the objector's) merits that counts.

Unanswered 'flaws' fester. They corrode your influence. It is necessary to GOYA and answer them. If the objections have substance, be thankful you found out before they found you out. And do not forget to thank the people who brought the problem to your attention, because there is nothing like acknowledgement for making opponents into allies.

ANSWERS TO SELF-ASSESSMENT TEST 16

1. (a) Yes.
   (b) No.
   (c) No.

2. (a) Least likely to succeed if its proponents are as committed

to their initiative as you are against it.

(b) More likely to succeed than (a) but depends on the lottery of arguments, including votes, about its merits.

(c) Most likely to succeed because it appeals to 'fairness', does not dismiss the initiative out of hand and, above all, delays the initiative starting until (exhaustive) studies are completed.

3. (a) 'Ambition should be made of sterner stuff' (Shakespeare, *Julius Caesar*). While a 68 per cent vote against you is indicative of opinion, it is not usually indicative of the intensity of feelings 'for' and 'against' something. You need more information.

(b) Yes. Half the opposition may be 'lukewarm' or opposed to only an aspect of your proposal. You have work to do, including, perhaps, adjusting your initiative to take account of the salient aspect worrying half the opposition. Bring them over and you have a majority.

(c) Not unless you have plenty of time and do not mind a reputation for fighting lost causes.

SELF-ASSESSMENT TEST 17

1. Occasionally you have to deal with someone who is absolutely obnoxious and upsetting to be with for any length of time and apparently he sees you in the same way. Do you:
   (a) ignore his behaviour and minimise your contact with him?
   (b) attempt to overcome your antipathy by every means available?
   (c) have a heart-to-heart talk with him to see why there is this mutual dislike?

2. You have been given new responsibilities in your organisation requiring you to liaise with people you have not met. Do you:
   (a) call them and arrange a meeting?
   (b) ask a friend who knows them to introduce you?
   (c) GOYA?

CHAPTER 17

Influencing for results

On your first day in your organisation, you knew nobody and, other than your interviewers, nobody knew you. You were a stranger in a strange environment.

It takes time to get to know with whom you have to deal to do your job. After a time you know many people from your interactions with (and in some cases, against) them.

On your first day, what is going on and who does what are a bewildering jumble. You are unlikely to feel involved because you are too new to be of much use. Such introductions as you receive are not likely to mean much or to be memorable, though you search for clues around you (unless, as I was at the UN Food and Agricultural Organisation some years ago, you are left all day with nothing to do and no contact with anybody at all, in a closed room with no windows; they 'forgot' I was there!).

So on your first day you 'know' only a few strange faces. You meet more and more people as you work, and the number you get to know grows.

You may come to regret some of the things you did in your early days, or how you reacted to some of the things done to you. You may also have failed to build relationships with people whom you have discovered since to be decisive to outcomes important to you.

It is time to take stock and audit your relationships because, make no mistake, your influencing potential determines your performance.

INFLUENCE OR BE INFLUENCED

Use your time and energy to meet your goals, or use them, unwittingly perhaps, to meet somebody else's. You are either a player or a pawn and, while a pawn's life can be quite comfortable (ignorance can be bliss), you perform well below your potential.

ACTIVITY 79

Think of the number of people you now know in your organisation.

Organisational theorists favour neatly drawn charts showing managerial and departmental titles. Their purpose is shrouded in mystery. Let's explore them by introducing some carefully chosen jargon as a prelude to an audit.

Functionaries are the people who make things happen – accountants account; sales staff sell; buyers buy; producers fabricate and so on. If you want something done, functionaries supposedly do it. Normally, you do not go to the secretarial service to arrange transport for your warehouse, or to buying to send sales staff to an exhibition. Knowing who is *supposed* to do what is the first step in your audit.

The second step is to identify those people among the functionaries whom you know well and who make it easier for you to do your job. You have established friendly relations with them ranging from the normal banter between the people you greet, gossip with and 'kid', to those with whom you have firm relationships (Chapter 9). These are your *potential allies,* towards whom you are broadly empathetic and, to a degree, they are to you.

The last step is to identify your *allies*: when they exert themselves on your behalf, things happen. They are strategic players and your most valuable resource.

ACTIVITY 80

Note three or four people you know whom you can place in each category (functionary, potential ally and ally).

Now complete the audit by allocating everybody in your organisation to one of the headings. Yes, I know this can be daunting, but do it anyway (taking care, of course, to keep your doodle in a safe place, preferably not at your workplace!). In equilibrium, the relationship between these three groups is shown in Figure 17.1

Everybody in the organisation is a functionary and this is the largest circle. Two smaller circles, for potential allies and allies, differ in size because it is presumed at this stage in your career that you have many more potential allies than allies. Many people with whom you have friendly contact will be in no position to give you direct help in your FAME.

For example, you may have potential allies in the mailroom – valid in itself – but they are not able to help you in a budgeting FAME with senior players much further up the power scale. The allies you need in FAME are a smaller group than your potential allies.

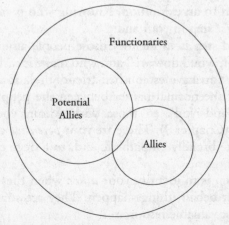

Figure 17.1: Equilibrium Status

The two overlapping circles represent the situation in FAME in which some of your allies are drawn from your pool of potential allies, but only on a temporary basis. The head of the mailroom, for example, could be a player (an ally) and some of her staff could be among your potential allies, but they might not be players, let alone allies, in FAME.

Obviously, recruiting a functionary of whom you know nothing as an ally is much more difficult than bringing a potential ally into play. Hence, the broad rule that drives relationship building is to keep in regular touch with functionaries throughout the organisation and recruit them as potential allies. Later, you develop your potential allies into allies.

FAME IMPERATIVES

To achieve an objective there are certain imperatives that must be met. An imperative can be political – adopt a policy, win an election, or secure a nomination. It can be commercial – reduce labour costs, enlarge market share, or raise prices. It can be related to people – recruit programmers, re-train electricians, or change supervision.

Imperatives must be achieved – like tactical objectives in a military campaign – in order to achieve the strategic objective.

For example, to raise profitability in your unit, the imperatives you select include reducing rework, trimming costs, improving productivity, getting people working together, and so on. Each imperative, if met, delivers your objective; if they are not met your objective isn't. Identifying the imperatives, therefore, is crucial.

Now identify the functionaries essential to each imperative. Who – and this must be personal – among the functionaries can deliver each imperative?

To reorganise distribution you need the co-operation of, say, the merchandising manager and her team. If only they can provide the specific information you need timeously then no information means no reorganisation. Delay an imperative and the objective is delayed: if it is not, it is not an imperative. Fudged imperatives compromise the objective.

Your objective may be a major or a minor change. In all but the most trivial of cases, you should prepare a balance of the forces for and against the change, covering all of the players, the arguments and the events relevant to each imperative and to the overall objective.

Identify each player by name. Names of departments, without the names of the players, advertise gaps in your preparation. Fabricated steelwork is not delivered to a site by 'transport'; it is delivered by supervised drivers, loaders and truck maintenance and repair people, who have names and locations (yes, you must GOYA!).

Alongside the names of functionaries, rank them as potential allies and allies. You could try coloured highlighter pens to aid rapid visualisation: say, yellow for potential allies; green for allies and red for the rest. A sea of red, or numerous red archipelagos, suggests that you have some way to go before you are ready to exert influence.

One useful device to survey your relationships with the players who are essential to achieve the tactical imperatives is shown in Figure 17.2. If you do not yet know some of the players, you had better remedy this deficiency.

Potential allies consist of both functionaries and those already inducted into the role of potential allies. You should systematically pass each one through the diagnostic process in Figure 17.2.

One approach to a functionary is to ask for their help (Chapter 4), followed by an intense course in relationship building, with heavy attention to fishing, wallowing and reframing (Chapters 9, 10, and 11). To develop your relationship from a potential ally, focus on doing good turns and avoiding bad turns (Chapter 9) and exchanging currencies (Chapter 13).

As functionaries become potential allies and potential allies become allies, apply FAME to those whom you require to play, not forgetting that 'while it don't take much to stay in touch' (Chapter 2), it is easy to lose touch through over-confidence or lethargy. You can run several FAMEs in parallel or sequence (Chapters 15 and 16), always remembering to remain focused on your objective.

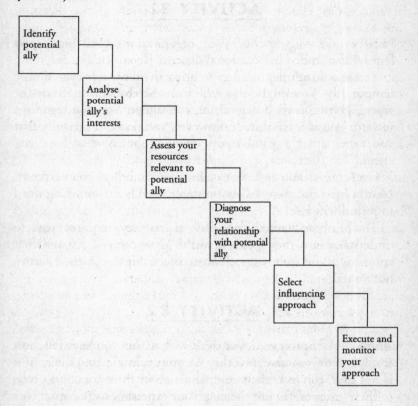

Figure 17.2 An Influencing Agenda for Potential Allies

Now some players may be among those with whom you have, to put it mildly, tense relationships. They are antagonistic or unsympathetic towards you because of events or your past carelessness. These casualties of your previous attempts at influence include rivals who regard you as a threat (organisations are not always ruled by 'sweetness and light': some are riven with dissent).

ACTIVITY 81

How would you describe your organisation? One big happy family? Embroiled in occasional dissent? Riven with strife?

You should adopt a strategy to bring them on-side even if only temporarily. You might also reflect on the costs of carelessly (or worse, gratuitously) antagonising colleagues. Some antagonism towards you is inevitable. If, however, you tread so carefully that you never upset anybody, you are too submissive to have any effect.

On some issues you have to take sides; on others you need not. Neutrality is not always dishonourable. Nor is a comforting word to prominent losers.

To bring someone into play as an ally requires you to understand how they see their world. How can you assuage their concerns about how your changes affect them – in their terms, not yours?

ACTIVITY 82

Think of the functionaries or rivals with whom you have the most trouble. Now rehearse how they see your role affecting theirs. If it is not easy, run over their complaints about your function's role, or their 'excuses' for not meeting your expectations (Chapter 6).

Many of the relationship-building techniques discussed in Chapters 9 to 12 are relevant here, though it is to be hoped you have them in play for some time prior to when you need allies. Influencers who only appear when they want something are as cynically received by allies and potential allies as politicians who only call on you when there is an election.

Certain individuals resolutely oppose you and no amount of effort on your part alters their disposition. Not everybody owes you their love and affection. Face it, some people can't stand the sight nor the sound of you. But it's no big deal because everybody annoys somebody. You do have problems if *everybody* can't stand the sight or sound of you!

ACTIVITY 83

Be candid: is there anyone in your organisation whom you cannot stand?

You can hope for their neutrality; more likely, if they actively campaign against your proposals or undermine their implementation, you may have to go head-to-head with them.

This problem is made worse only if relations between yourself and those who oppose you deteriorate to the point that they damage the organisation's effectiveness. When this happens, the CEO is likely to take drastic action against both of you. To prevent this happening (in your interests) avoid personalising disputes. Once a functional clash personalises, it usually spirals out of control.

If tempted to personalise a dispute, or when watching one developing between others, recollect the ultimate personalisation of a dispute: that between the Brazilian Navy and the Airforce some years back. Briefly, the navy acquired an aircraft carrier but the airforce insisted on the planes remaining part of the airforce. The navy argued that planes on an aircraft carrier belonged to the navy. The dispute got so bad that, in an ultimate outburst of personal antipathy (or 'madness'), the airforce ended up trying to bomb the aircraft carrier! So, think 'aircraft carrier' before you enter into personality clashes. Otherwise, you might be 'bombed' by your boss.

You need allies to get the job done. So begin to cultivate potential allies long before you need them. If they are needed for specific projects, identify who they are, how they see 'their world' (not yours), and what you can do yourself and through third parties to develop your relationships (think 'wallowing').

The very qualities in players that draw you to them are usually the same qualities that draw them to you. Expand your potential allies across the organisation and at all levels. Help them where you can and seek opportunities to demonstrate your benign intentions (avoid instances where a malign interpretation of your behaviour is possible). Listen sympathetically to their accounts of their 'adversities' and joyously celebrate accounts of their triumphs.

And do not put a verbal gloss on what you hear from them to third parties. Joe was 'not moaning again' – he was 'disappointed'; George was not 'smirking' – he was 'happy'. The language you use about others when you think it is safe to be frank, damages you if your third-party 'confidant' spreads it about as confirmation of their own prejudiced opinions and it gets back to your (ex-)ally. When reframing, always be positive.

ANSWERS TO SELF-ASSESSMENT TEST 17

1. (a) Probably your best response and what you will have to do if (b) and (c) fail.
   (b) Sounds ethical but in practice is usually a tinge self-justificatory.
   (c) Probably the one thing that makes matters worse. People have a right to choose whom they like or dislike.

2. (a) Failing (b).
   (b) Preferably, but if not possible, try (a), then (c).
   (c) Try (b), then (a) and follow up smartly with a GOYA.

CHAPTER 18

Influencing with power

So far our approach is best defined as influencing *without* power, or how to influence when you have neither power nor authority (or at least, not much of either) over the people you wish to influence. By extension, it is assumed that by reading *Influencing for Results* you wish to consider how to acquire the power or authority you presently lack.

Another approach is to study how people in powerful positions in organisations, including corporations, political parties, government departments, inter-governmental agencies and suchlike, use the extensive power they have acquired to influence those with whom they interact, both formally and informally, for their organisation's (and personal) goals.

One of the leading exponents of the influence *with* power approach is Jeffrey Pfeffer (*Managing with Power: politics and influence in organisations*, Harvard, 1992). In fact, Pfeffer's title neatly defines the basic difference between the two approaches. Pfeffer, and other exponents of the managing with power approach, observe how powerful men and women exert influence, how they acquire more power and thereby more influence, and how, sometimes, they lose their power and with it their influence. This approach is backed by a formidable body of research, plus a rich field of commentary, biography and autobiography of the world's most powerful players. Being celebrities, the powerful have attracted a ready audience for their memoirs and 'secrets'.

In this last chapter, we examine how power is a source of

influence and how powerful people influence their organisations, or influence the situations in which they operate.

Necessarily, the style I use is slightly more formal and if you find this tiresome, you should skip it for now and start applying the methods outlined in Chapters 1 to 17. You can always come back to this chapter once you have you have thrown a double six in your influencing career, either to see what you are missing or to see what you are about to miss if your next throw sends you down a snake and not up a ladder.

POWER

Power has many definitions. My preferred definition is:

> Power is the ability to make someone do what they otherwise would not (or stop them doing what they otherwise would).

This definition incorporates the overt effect of power on people, who are affected sufficiently to commence or desist certain behaviours.

Examples of overt power are when employees are instructed to commence new work schedules or to desist from smoking near hazardous chemicals. Power is transmitted by enforcing obedience to an instruction.

An example of the covert effect of power is when an employee does not pursue a harassment case because she persuades herself that it is not in her best interests, or where she holds back from seeking promotion because she believes the selectors prefer another person. No visible instruction, warning or threat is transmitted to her – she submits of her own volition.

ACTIVITY 84

Have you experienced covert power in forgoing something important to you? Did you forgo, say, applying for a promotion or a post in another company, because you believed the odds were stacked against you?

Power is not an entity in itself. It is always an interdependent relationship: it expresses itself through people who are dependent on each other to varying degrees. A charismatic leader without followers is redundant (which was the fate of poor old Napoleon on St Helena).

The study of power is dominated by myriad citations of John French and Bertram Raven's famous five sources of power:

Legitimate	the right of authority
Reward	an ability to reward
Coercive	an ability to punish
Referent	intrinsic qualities, such as charisma
Expert	specialised 'know-how'

Legitimacy as a source of power is not effective in all contexts. Having the right to order someone to do something does not guarantee that they will do it (as you will find out in your first supervisory post – or when you first try to ride a horse, or herd some cats).

Authority is not the same as power because a conferred right does not necessarily ensure any ability to exercise the right. If people comply with your instructions you can be said to have legitimised your right to instruct; if they do not comply, your legitimacy is in question. For example, you may legitimately order your sales team to increase sales by 10 per cent and if they try to do so they confirm your legitimacy; if they do not try at all they demonstrate your lack of legitimacy.

ACTIVITY 85

Do you have legitimacy of any kind that gives you power? Are you, for example, a parent? Have you tried instructing newborn babies to go to sleep?

Reward power enables people to exert influence by virtue of their ability to reward those who obey them. A sales manager who awards bonuses to staff for exceeding quantitative sales targets has considerable influence over the behaviour of those staff who desire a bonus, as does a manager who conducts appraisal interviews with employees whose appraisals affect their salary progressions.

ACTIVITY 86

Do you have reward power in your job? How do you exercise it? Does somebody have reward power over you?

Conversely, the power to punish matches the power to reward. Withholding a reward punishes; actively imposing sanctions to ensure someone's compliance coerces. People who coerce others have discretion to punish.

An employee assigned by a supervisor to do routine, boring and repetitive tasks, week after week, and who is denied access to more interesting work, may be coerced into altering his behaviour (or, more likely, quitting).

ACTIVITY 87

What coercive power do you experience in your job? Have you ever felt a supervisor was picking on you coercively? Have you ever bullied somebody into submission?

Referent power is about the perceived characteristics associated with an individual by those who are influenced by him or her. Charisma is one such example (as is any aspect of that elusive quality, leadership).

Being 'much respected', 'highly regarded', 'a safe pair of hands' and so on, can clinch a bid for promotion in a crisis. Referent power is the often intangible and inherent quality of the individual that gives him or her power and influence over others, much as the reputation for some quality (probity and integrity) is considered useful for certain tasks.

ACTIVITY 88

Have you worked for anyone who has referent power? Could you specify something about the form it took and how you and others recognised it?

Expert power is more tangible than referent power and is subject to evidence. 'Red' Adair's reputation grew from extinguishing fires in oil wells. Airline pilots have expert power evidenced by tough training and continuous re-examination of their flying skills. Data processing managers, in the early days of business computing, wielded significant expert power over their non-expert colleagues by monopolising the understanding of the technology and what it could do, and their ability to deal with experts from IBM, Digital and Hewlett-Packard on an expert-to-expert basis.

ACTIVITY 89

What expert power do you have and could you develop it as an influencing tool?

Looking through French and Raven's list, notice that some of their sources of power are mutually reinforcing. For example, an army general, such as George Patton, had significant legitimate power as a commander in the US Army and, as significant, referent power from his extraordinary charisma. He also had expert power from his professional competence in waging war. His legitimate power was supported by reward and coercion power – he could promote and demote those around him. (He was himself punished for an incident in which he exercised illegitimate coercive power in lightly assaulting a soldier whom he perceived to be a malingerer.)

Sources of power may conflict. A person who exercises legitimate power (from holding a position in a hierarchy) can provoke resistance to his influence by unfairly exercising coercive power – the fate of Lieutenant William Bligh, commander of HMS *Bounty*, in 1789. In contrast, commanders such as Captain James Cook and Admiral Lord Nelson, who exercised significant influence over their subordinates, despite being tougher disciplinarians than Lieutenant Bligh, compensated for their excessive coercive power with extraordinary charismatic referent power.

ACTIVITY 90

Does anybody you know combine different sources of power or compensate between them?

The five sources of power identified by French and Raven are not exhaustive. We can add emotional sources of power, and thereby, of influence, from such qualities as love, friendship, comradeship (especially in situations of shared high stress or danger), solidarity and loyalty. These emotional qualities can so bind together the people they affect that extraordinary self-sacrifices are possible from subordinates, even at the cost of their lives. A senior manager in the oil industry once remarked to me (almost with regret) that no management was ever able to exert such 'tyrannical' discipline upon employees as their union leaders when they acted collectively against the company.

There are other sources of power, notably positional power, in which power and influence originate from occupying a crucial position in an organisation (which, at first glance, may not appear important). Positional power is not the same as the power of legitimacy (power accorded to the holder of a rank or title) because positional power comes from controlling key resources, though the position may be relatively low in the formal hierarchy (Chapter 3).

Chairmen of key committees, who control what and when something appears on the agenda, exert enormous influence, particularly during a controversy. Some key committees, such as

Ways and Means in the US Congress, provide relevant examples of positional power. And it is not only the formal head of a committee who exercises influence over others. Membership of a committee may be sufficient, particularly in those with a 'lazy' or less energetic head nominally in charge.

ACTIVITY 91

Are you a member of a key committee of any kind, or could you seek to join such a committee? What key committees would provide you with positional power if you could become a member?

Remuneration committees exert great influence over the members of the main board because the committee decides on the all-important amounts of salary, the size of share options and the amounts that may be granted for golden handcuffs (to retain) and golden parachutes (to terminate). Similarly with budgetary committees processing applications for funds and staffing committees allocating promotions and recruitment.

So the possibility that power, emanating from multiple sources and in different combinations, exerts influence and that relationships between people also influence their behaviours, suggests that the links between influence and power are as complex as they are interesting.

Such links are subject to changes, prominent among which has been the erosion of deference in society over recent decades. Hierarchies have flattened, some dramatically, and previously highly regarded positions in organisations no longer attract the same degree of deference (as their holders discover literally minutes after they quit or are terminated when the chauffeur-driven Jaguar is withdrawn).

NO FAVOURS FOR HIRED HELP

A famous movie star was invited to London to discuss a leading role in a multimillion-dollar movie. He was flown by private jet to Heathrow, where a chauffeur-driven Rolls-Royce met him and drove him to Soho to meet the producers. After much low-key haggling, he signed the contract to do the part for $10 million. The producer left the room with the signed contract, but did not return.

A secretary eventually came in and handed him a large envelope. She asked if he wanted a taxi to take him to the airport. She said nothing about the Rolls. Mildly put out by this, he took the taxi and searched the envelope for his private pass to the private jet to take him back to Geneva. It only contained his copy of the contract. He had to pay for the taxi too, which left him at the VIP entrance.

He rang the producer but he had left for New York (probably in the Rolls). He asked the secretary where she had put his pass to the VIP lounge. She replied that employees bought and paid for their own tickets home, quoting the clause in the contract, and advised him to enquire in Terminal 2 and buy a ticket. He could only claim in arrears for expenses on location and they were not shooting for six months. In the meantime all costs were his own.

The next commercial flight was fully booked but he managed a cancellation in economy class. He wondered if they treated the real James Bond like this?

This loss of respect for those at the top of hierarchies – the 'establishment' – is not caused solely by cynicism, though this is a contributory element. Across all organisations and institutions, authority and with it legitimacy has declined. Paternal domination has declined in the basic family unit (as has the number of the traditional family unit of two married parents with 1.8 children).

ACTIVITY 92

Ask anybody over 50 about the changes they have noticed between their upbringing in a traditional family ('children are seen and not heard') and what they think of the way their grandchildren are brought up or, better still, ask them what they think of the way other people's grandchildren are brought up, particularly in the area of discipline.

Legislative protection of children's rights in the home and at school reflects the consequences of the widespread behavioural changes spreading across society. Where parental authority once was enough to ensure compliant behaviour from children (backed occasionally by low-level coercive intervention), it is now more common for adults to use various non-authoritarian inducements to promote acceptable behaviour from children in their charge.

Legitimacy is probably less of a source of power and influence than it was and in some contexts it may be counterproductive. A single, unarmed, police officer in the past might have prevented a crime by being present and visible at the scene; today, he or she has more chance of becoming a victim.

The unilateral discretionary powers of managers are now constrained. Legislation to protect employees from unfair and arbitrary dismissal, tyrannical or unsafe work practices, harassment of various kinds, pay cuts and extensions to hours of work or attendance, weakens the power of managers to use promises of reward or threats of sanction to influence the behaviour of employees.

And beyond the legal protection of employees, a large part of the reward and coercive apparatus, once controlled by supervisors, has been passed to committees of managers who operate strict procedures for changing individual remuneration, selecting for promotion or demotion and the allocation of duties.

Managers, to exercise reward or punishment powers have to persuade, influence or negotiate with colleagues where once their discretion was near absolute. This weakens the reward and coercive basis of managerial power exercised by individuals and passes it to small groups.

ACTIVITY 93

In your organisation, who decides budgetary, disciplinary, remuneration and promotion issues? Is it (unlikely) a single person or (more commonly) committees?

Increasing and more complex information flows are changing the shape of management structures. In place of top-down hierarchies, there are mutually dependent centres of decision-making. Managers get things done through other people who bring to the process their expertise. These managers need to interact formally and informally to process their information into the group decision. Interpersonal skills, primarily influencing and communication are at a premium at all levels in the modern organisation because managers increasingly are dependent on the co-operative goodwill of each other.

Changes in the bases of power – for example less deference, less respect for authority, greater division of expertise into smaller units of information which is quickly outdated, and lower reliance on referent qualities in leadership – have increased the role of influencing strategies because of the wider reliance on groups in decision-making.

Where groups thrive, politics proliferate.

POLITICS

One interesting way of looking at politics in an organisation is shown in Figure 18.1, which represents the distribution of managers along two dimensions: their political awareness and their scruples.

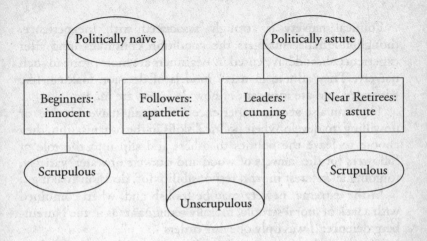

Figure 18.1 Politicians in an Organisation

ACTIVITY 94

In which box (Figure 18.1) would you place yourself?

Managers may be politically naïve or politically astute and all points in between.

Former US Secretary of State, Henry Kissinger, confessed his political naïvety before he experienced high-level politics:

> Before I served as a consultant to Kennedy, I had believed, like most academics, that the process of decision-making was largely intellectual and all one had to do was to walk into the President's office and convince him of the correctness of one's view. This perspective I soon realised was as dangerously immature as it is widely held (*The White House Years*, Kissinger, Little, Brown, Boston, 1979).

Kissinger, of course, learned his craft fast and became one of the most astute of political managers in post-war American government.

Political naïvety is strongly associated with inexperience, though for many mangers the condition continues long after experience should have cured it. Beginners are most prone to such naïvety. They adhere to naïve models of decision-making, like Kissinger, and are innocent of how decisions are made.

They can also acquire experience and remain naïve. Unable, or unwilling, to develop their political skills in the organisation, they choose to leave the politics to others and slip into the role of followers (of the 'hewers of wood and drawers of water' variety), forgoing all interest in, and responsibility for, decision-making.

In the extreme, naïvety may be foolish and, when combined with a lack of moral scruple, morally repugnant (as in the Nuremberg defence: 'I was only obeying orders').

The scrupulous–unscrupulous dimension is the second definer of political behaviour. To what extent is the manager guided by scruples? The young, inexperienced person tends to idealism and unchallenged (and innocent) scruples. The experienced manager's scruples have been tested by events and by the twin temptations of ambition and convenience.

Political astuteness is associated with experience, though some learn from their experience a lot faster than others and a few keep repeating the errors they learned early on, which they call 'experience'.. The truly experienced practise their politics in the prime of their managerial careers.

ACTIVITY 95
·

Which are you most like: truly experienced (run through some of your early errors!), or poorly experienced, because you merely repeat your early errors?

The truly experienced know 'where the bodies are buried' (they helped to 'bury' some of them). They know how decisions are made and how to get others to do what they want done, cunningly using all the artifices of political manipulation at their disposal. They exercise influence through the judicious use of power over colleagues and followers. They share with followers a willingness to disregard or suspend the scruples that others profess to uphold. They 'get the job done' – whatever the collateral damage to their relationships.

ACTIVITY 96

Consider your own organisation and assess which of its managers you would describe as politically astute. Are there many of them?

When powerful managers pass their prime and approach retirement (not having been caught out before then) they pass from a tendency to ruthless unscrupulousness to a sort of rediscovery of long-forgotten scruples. They become astute but not naïve.

The near retirees still make things happen in the organisation – especially in a crisis – but mostly they remain above the fray. They no longer feel the passion that they once had for the battle. They tend to be dismissed by subordinate rivals as 'no longer up to it' and they suffer from moves to remove them or to 'kick 'em upstairs'. The politically astute manager, who knows when she has passed her best bows out gracefully. Some try to carry on as if nothing has changed, which may be a mistake if their business has changed fundamentally as a result of technological developments or new rivals entering their markets. If they fail to recognise these changes, they will be swept aside by those who out-play them in the political games at which they once excelled.

ACTIVITY 97

Has this happened in any organisation you know of in your experience? How did it play out? Was the manager pushed or did he jump?

Arrogance, over-confidence, defiance and irrelevant memories of past victories over rivals are so common in the political end-games that signal the demise of the men and women who outstayed their welcome, that it is a wonder that so many wise, experienced and capable people suffer the public ignominy of a boardroom coup. If they did suspect that the writing was on the wall, why did they not quit while they were still ahead? Were they merely hanging on until they were offered a lucrative severance package?

POLITICAL ACTIVITY

If the degree of a person's political awareness is an indicator of their political activity, to what extent can you identify the behaviours of the political activist?

Management literature differentiates between 'High Machs' and 'Low Machs'. These categories do not exhaust the possible ranges of political activity but they provide a swift way into a confusing and complex terminology.

'Mach' refers to the sixteenth-century Italian political thinker, Niccolò Machiavelli, whose books, *The Prince* (1513) and the *Discourses* (1515), are still in print. They continue to generate controversy and Machiavelli's name is associated in popular comment with political manipulation, intrigue and amoral behaviour.

Machiavelli worked at the heart of the Florentine court and wrote about the behaviour of rulers in fifteenth- and sixteenth-century Italy. He was the first political scientist and was dispassionately interested in how rulers ('princes') held and lost power.

Several top managers of my acquaintance claim they used Machiavelli's *Prince* in their rise to the top – one showed me his battered copy from a drawer in his office desk – though this may have been mere boasting. The fact is that Machiavelli's image (more so than his actual writings) is well established in influencing studies.

Richard Christie and Florence Geis (*Studies in Machiavellianism*, Academic Press, New York 1970, described 'High

Machs' as people with a manipulative orientation, who are cool, emotionally detached and 'logically' (by their own standards) oriented. Allegedly they act in disregard of their feelings and of the feelings of others. Their behaviour is summarised in the popular notion that 'the end justifies the means'. High Machs also believe that they are the masters of their destiny and that they alone are responsible for what happens to themselves. People, by contrast, who complain about their personal fate, in the view of a High Mach, are pathetic figures, unworthy of sympathy.

'Low Machs' are the opposite. Emotionally involved in what they do, they hold to ethical principles and codes, and are affected by their feelings and the feelings of others. Low Machs subscribe to the view that 'the means determine the end' and would never justify evil or immoral means to achieve even a worthy end.

They also see their personal destinies as something determined by forces outside of their control or influence. They accept being a victim of the behaviours of others.

ACTIVITY 98

Who would you say in your organisation is a High Mach?

The nature of an organisation influences the way High and Low Machs thrive. Highly structured organisations (traditional bureaucracies, for instance) are not conducive to High Mach behaviours, because employees have to work within the system according to the rules, regulations and restrictions. In contrast, Low Machs can do well in such organisations because they are comfortable working with rules and constraints determined by others.

Organisations with limited formal or bureaucratic structures are far looser, open, adaptive and flexible than their highly structured counterparts. High Machs thrive in such circumstances, while low Machs are ineffective and uncomfortable in coping with ambiguity.

Parenthetically, you should note that in practice highly

structured organisations are not devoid of politics. My own observations of the behaviour of men and women employed at the top of three tightly structured organisations – the Co-operative Movement, the National Health Service and the Police Force – suggest they operate in very political environments, certainly in matters of strategy and the all-important question of succession.

ACTIVITY 99

How about your organisation? Is it political or non-political?

Succession politics dominates the traditional bureaucratic organisation as much as the less structured – it just takes a different form! Being adept at the slower and more regularised game of succession is a political skill at and near the top in the highly structured organisations I have observed and it is every bit as demanding as rising rapidly in a low-structured organisation.

For one thing, High Machs, assuming they can sustain their interest for long enough, have to play very hard at pretending to have all the attributes of Low Machs, if they are to succeed all the way to the top in a bureaucratic organisation.

Observation suggests that disguising one's inherent Machiavellianism (and its amoral tones) in the tight confines of a bureaucratic regime for long periods without detection is extremely difficult and demanding. This supposedly gives the political advantage to the genuine Low Machs, but cunning and well-camouflaged High Machs who seek high office can do just as well.

Another explanation, of course, and one that has made me uneasy about the High/Low Mach distinction in the context of structured and unstructured organisations, is that people are not fixed in their propensities for High and Low Mach behaviours and that when the stakes are high enough, even Low Machs can switch into bouts of High Mach behaviour.

Becoming Chief Executive – or Chief Constable – is no mean political task. Similarly, it is observable that key players – the founders, no less – in loose, quasi-anarchistic businesses (Apple Computers?) suffer the consequences of their political blind spots – even naïvety. They leave the finances – and the politics – to their accountants.

How would we expect High Machs to behave? What tactics would they follow? In what way would you recognise what they were doing?

Generalising, High Machs keep their emotional distance from those around them and do not get too involved with colleagues. They do just enough to ingratiate themselves with potential sponsors above them and to create dependency relationships with potential protégés around and below them. If they become too close, they might have difficulty ditching someone who becomes an embarrassment to them.

For example, a decision to close a department that is run by a close friend may be difficult to execute – or to remain passive about – if emotional issues intrude. Indeed, for the High Mach to win the confidence of upper management, it could be essential to be assigned to execute the decision, or to be seen to support it.

Many a new personnel manager expresses doubts about the efficacy of a particular policy; some (Low Machs?) resign. Most overcome their doubts. They realise that they will never initiate their alternative policies if they do not get promoted to the positions of the people who initiate the policies with which they disagree.

Avoiding close friendships is accompanied by highly selective choices of people with whom to share decision-making. If colleagues do not need to know they are not told by the High Mach.

Confining decision-making to a tight group keeps it under control and protects the High Mach from unforeseen events, such as an unwelcome consensus influenced by rivals or random and maverick outsiders. Also, participative democracy does not fit the image of bold and confident leadership that the High Mach strives to project.

Penury in information sharing is also practised, at least from the High Mach to others. Receiving information from others and storing it until it might be fruitful to pass it on is commonplace. Basically, the High Mach strives to receive more information than he or she shares.

Joining a function in the organisation that has a future is a classic sign of a High Mach at work. So is joining a moribund department that can be used to gain leverage to a better position in the future. A moribund department is not the same as a declining function. A department may be moribund because it is not performing to its potential under the current leadership. A declining function may be terminally declining with no hope of recovery.

Consider the great film studio companies in Hollywood towards the end of their Golden Era, following the advent of television. High Machs who joined television production as it was taking off towards its mass consumer base made great careers, acquired a future for themselves and gained high net worth. As the old studios declined – there were too many producers (some with impeccable credentials as High Machs) with not enough money – jobs, careers and personal fortunes waned. While the studios declined, their film libraries were moribund. Those who spotted the difference made fortunes by acquiring control of the libraries and selling or leasing their old films to television stations desperately short of programmes to fill their time slots.

One caveat about joining a growing department with a glowing future is the old adage that all that glitters is not gold. What looks impressive and thereby tempting may turn out a disaster (Chapter 14).

A prominent characteristic of High Mach behaviour is what I call the gift of mimicry. High Machs are able to mimic convincingly expressions of the beliefs, attitudes and behaviours – and even the lifestyle codes – of those above and around them.

I know of a major bank that for many years had a senior cohort of managers in one of its three divisions, who all professed avidly to support the same football team, while in another division everybody at and near the top seemed inclined to be keen rugby fans. This may have been accidental, though because the situation changed with retirements and resignations over a seven-year period, I am inclined to think it was not.

INFLUENCING WITH POWER

Power is exercised by various means which serve to badge those who exercise power. The Chief Executive has a chauffeur-driven limousine. Various grades of employee, who require a car for their job function, are permitted to drive certain models only.

I once recommended to a poorly performing company a sales bonus system that would give all staff who reached enhanced sales targets the right to a company Mercedes. Though the model was the basic Mercedes 200, and though it would cost less than the Ford Granada saloon to which they were entitled (I checked with a dealer), and though the sales director acknowledged that the image of having a Mercedes would really fire up his people, it was knocked back by the then beleaguered soon to be ex-CEO because he was 'the only one going to drive a Mercedes in this company'.

Such power symbols exercise enormous influence on their holders and on those who aspire to high office. Office size, furnishings, views, privacy and other perquisites can take on a ridiculous relative importance.

Strict codes are enforced to ensure that managers know their place in the hierarchy and that their place is known to everybody who knows the code. In some offices certain people have international dialling from their phones, others have bars on anything but local calls, while others stretch across their desks to share phones. Some have carpets, some don't and some have meeting tables and chairs beside their desks and some share their desks ('hot desking').

Many firms now have open plan offices that ostensibly eliminate visible status differences. I was in a company recently where the entire operation, offices, stores and workshop, was open plan. It suggested an 'open hierarchy' without status symbols. Some acquaintance with the company soon showed that while the symbols of status were absent, the managerial style of the top managers was unusually autocratic, which conflicted with the 'democratic' layout of their offices.

If location is important in retail shopping, it is more important in influencing with power. A senior manager who locates physically distant from the building where the other senior managers operate close to the CEO, risks being sidelined as the company evolves. Even location on a separate floor in the same building has a deleterious effect on the exercise of influence. A senior manager, promoted to the board, and who elected to remain in the building where his department was run from and not in the same corridor as the other directors in the head office building two miles way, missed out on the informal, unscheduled and *ad hoc* discussions engaged in by his colleagues and rivals. This was taken as a lack of total commitment to the company and to nobody's surprise he left soon for other pastures.

All things being equal, location is important in building alliances and in containing threats to an executive's power base. If an executive is in power by the grace and favour of a powerful player, that dependency will condition the exercise of the executive's power.

Dependency is a source for transmitting support and power players look for opportunities to enhance their own power by making less powerful players dependent. Seeking opportunities requires contact, and location is a factor in facilitating contact.

POSITIONAL POWER

Jeffrey Pfeffer calls this the Golden Rule ('the person with the gold makes the rules'): namely that the person who controls the resources others want to access, exercises enormous influence, sometimes way above their formal station.

Examples of using positional power to generate influence are extremely common. They show how influencers use such power to generate more influence and also why some managers who neglect their positional power have little influence beyond the boundaries of their desk.

Take a city council which spends revenues from local taxes to provide public services to the community. Voters elect councillors to supervise the employees of the council who provide the services. Councillors serve four-year terms and if re-elected might serve until they retire. The employees of the council, once hired and subject only to their reasonable behaviour and continuing health, serve until retirement or seek employment elsewhere at their sole discretion.

How does informal influence work in practice? It certainly is not recorded in any official minutes nor in anybody's job descriptions. And be clear, I am not referring to instances or habits of personal corruption. Influence for personal monetary gain is illegal. Many people exercise enormous influence without graft and are more interested in accumulating power to extend influence than in accumulating mere money.

Councils divide their budgets among such services as education, roads, parking, sanitation, buildings, refuse collection, planning consents, parks, policing and housing. The public officials, often with a chief executive in overall charge, who manage these services are supervised by committees of elected members. The people who control the departments that supply the services use their positional power to gain influence.

The main goal of an elected politician is to be re-elected. The main goal of public officials is to protect their jobs. True, both have many sub-goals, such as gaining favourable publicity, protecting their department's budgets, hiring more staff, avoiding scandals, etc.

If politicians fall out with an official this could threaten the official's job; if an official maladministers a service, the electors could vote out of office any politician they regard as responsible for the failure in the service. Therefore, politicians and officials who are interested in each other's welfare strive to protect each other's interests.

The official in charge of the maintenance and repair of the council's roads, for example, does not have unlimited discretion over the roads budget. He or she does have discretion over day-to-day operations and there are usually more demands on the budget than can be accommodated. Potholes, eroded tarmac, weathered markings, awkward corners, dangerous cambers and suchlike are the stuff of local positional politics. Councillors are judged by how effective they are at removing these problems and the electors' expectations increase with the duration of the problem. Roads that need repairs create opportunities for influence. Roads officials exploit these opportunities by the 'fortuitous' creation of 'extra' resources – work gangs, equipment, materials and spare budgets – which they 'squeeze' out of limited budgets by their 'good management' and offer to politicians harassed by their electors for immediate action.

In effect, officials 'buy' political protection from politicians, who benefit from their discretionary support when the officials remove actual or potential electoral liabilities for them.

ACTIVITY 100

Is there apparent collusion between officials and local politicians in your area?

Players who can gain control of resources – the 'golden rule' – exercise power disproportionately. In a trade union, the official who controls the votes of the largest branch effectively controls the executive.

An ambitious and energetic union officer in the UK built up the union's branch at a local airport so successfully that when the then national negotiator resigned before the end of his term, he was unstoppable as a candidate for appointment as the new national negotiator, even though there were several older and more experienced rivals above him.

In a university, for example, the 'gold' is the budget, almost entirely contributed by government funding and research grants (mainly from public bodies). Large departments of long standing exert more influence than small departments with expensive requirements. New disciplines have a hard time establishing themselves, unless government policy changes and favours them. These budgetary realities have little to do with worth, competence or student demand. Coalitions of other departments prevent the growth of departments where student demand for places is high (accountancy, law and business) by imposing quotas on their student numbers, even if the admission of more of these students, and less of some other traditional disciplines, would raise the average academic quality of the university. It is not, of course, a rational decision but a protective decision by those likely to receive less from the budget.

If, however, a department can gain funding from outside government sources, it can break a coalition holding it back. If such funding comes fully fungible and free of restrictions upon what it can be spent, that department is able to exert disproportionate influence on the university. It can also break up the former coalitions that were against it.

The 'gold' does not have to be money. It can be promotions, recruitment, resources, facilities, visibility and the many 'currencies' discussed in Chapter 13. Their disbursement works on the reciprocity principle. In an organisation where decisions on these issues are made by interlocking committees, it is essential that the players who seek influence get themselves, or their dependent allies, on to these committees.

Membership of committees is a chore to most people and the reluctance to do the chore assiduously provides gaps in the structure through which power bases can be built.

Powerful people have influence to the extent that they 'know' everybody that matters (and many that don't) and they know whom to call (GOTT) or visit (GOYA), who will invariably return their calls or find time to see them. Communication networks in an organisation, formal and informal, are well-traversed territories for people with, and searching for, power.

Influential managers have powerful associates. They meet formally within the organisation's communication structure and also informally on a semi-social level. Watch with whom they lunch or socialise after work. Because they mix with the powerful, they appear to be powerful themselves by implicit association (a point noted by the ambitious). This means spending a considerable amount of time socialising with people they do not particularly like (compared to others with whom they could party) and participating in social activities that would not be their first choice in entertainment. Their willingness to endure some of these events, and the people that go with them, is part of the price they pay to obtain and exercise influence.

A willingness to execute tough decisions and see them through against opposition is a decisive requirement for the powerful influencer. The tough decision can be a policy issue – a major change in direction – or a personnel problem, including removing a serious rival from contention in the hierarchy. Successfully executing tough decisions powerfully confirms a person's influence and a reputation for success reinforces their claim to power. Conversely, a failure in either respect – to carry through the tough decision or to successfully implement it – can break a career.

Machiavelli warned that it was not good enough to 'wound the Prince' because a wounded Prince could fight back. He had to be removed, permanently. Because people are closely bound up with policies, defeating the person usually means defeating the policy (and vice versa). Boardroom battles over policy issues or between people usually amount to the same thing. If a major policy has to be defeated, the people behind the policy have to go too.

Recent board-level battles are representative of what can be at stake and of the typical tactics employed to secure victory. These vary from the relatively underhand to the almost benign, though equally decisive. Underhand tactics include meeting without the target person present and securing the votes to dismiss him or her before the formal meeting. One CEO realised his time was up when he was called to an emergency board meeting late at night and found everybody present, amidst visible signs that they had been meeting for some time without him – the side tables had trays of food and dirty dishes piled on them and the board table was strewn with papers in a typical post-meeting disorder.

Another example was when a firm's bankers called a meeting with the chairman and a majority of the board for 11 a.m., when they knew full well that the leading advocate of avoiding a takeover was driving to a meeting 50 miles away on board business. Notice of the emergency meeting was sent to his home by messenger and timed to arrive forty-five minutes after he had left for his appointment. By the time his wife telephoned him at the office he had driven to, the emergency board meeting was over and the hostile takeover accepted by his colleagues on pain of the bank putting the company into liquidation.

Trade union leaders can be as ruthless as capitalists in removing opposition. A union leader on sick leave was spotted at a holiday resort by a colleague. His colleague, who owed his own prominence in the union to the patronage of the 'sick' leader, reported his former mentor to the union's executive, which voted to suspend him from office. In the ensuing election his whistle-blowing colleague was voted in as the new leader.

Other attempted coups that go wrong – the votes to dismiss fail to carry the day – result in the challengers themselves having to resign or falling victim of a counter-coup. Sniping from the sidelines, dithering when push comes to shove, or incompetently pressing the attack, leads to career crashes.

CONCLUDING REMARKS

Influencing attempts are not for the faint-hearted! They do not always – if ever – operate in benign environments only. There are choices to be made, many of which carry risks, and the wrong choices create self-inflicted and unintended setbacks.

Dithering between choices is not an option. This is why FAME players always make 'reality checks' with confidants and allies before they make irreversible choices.

Don't dismiss this advice out of hand.

Remember, in influencing you are not the lone ranger. You need players on your side, including people perfectly qualified to play the parts of the 'fools you suffer gladly', at least until you can get shot of them by your success. Of course, not all players are fools. The main thing to ensure is that you don't become one, by ignoring good advice (and not seeking it is the first sign of a fool) or by playing good advice badly.

Stars rapidly rising in the firmament as rapidly crash back to earth. Many seek influence and many fewer exercise it. Those who fail were not all fools – some were very, very good. But if they had a flaw, it was almost certainly that they forgot that the instruments of their sought-for success were other people, and not their own genius or their superiority over lesser mortals.

The chain breaks at the weakest link, and in influencing the weakest link might well be you – especially if you keep thinking the weakest links are among the people around you.

Two mountaineers climbing a rock face, each thinking they are world class compared to the other and who forget they are joined together by the same ropes, might be reminded by neutral nature that, while it is tremendously difficult to climb to the top, it is incomparably easier to fall back down. Such fatal ends often emanate from the simplest of errors.

If, despite this sketch of the possible futures for you when you play in the big league, you still want to try for it – good luck (though don't trust to it!).

You know what you have to do – for a start, you just have to GOYA!

Appendix 1:
HELPLINE for readers to consult the author (free service)

With the purchase of *Influencing for Results* you are entitled to send to my HELPMAIL service one of your influencing problems and, provided you pay for the postage (mine included!) your first use of the Negotiate HELPMAIL service is absolutely FREE of charge!

But please, do not try to use the HELPMAIL service via the telephone because over-eager beavers would soon clog up my phone lines and prevent my conduct of Negotiate's business in a professional manner.

The more relevant the detail you include in your HELPMAIL the more effective my response, but please do not send original documents for which no responsibility for safe keeping is accepted (photocopies are more than adequate). My comments will be confined to the influencing aspects of the problems only. I do not offer legal, financial or technical advice, for which you must consult the relevant licensed professionals. All correspondence will be treated confidentially and will not be disclosed to third parties (but influencing problems of an illegal or unethical nature will be declined and the materials shredded).

Please send a self-addressed envelope with an International Postal Coupon for the same amount that it costs you to send your material to me. The postal address for the HELPMAIL service is:

HELPMAIL
99 Caiyside
Edinburgh
EH10 7HR
Scotland
UK

You may also send your material by e-mail to: <gavin@negotiate.demon.co.uk> marked 'For the Attention of HELPMAIL' (otherwise for legal reasons I cannot respond).

Disclaimer:
The HELPMAIL service is confined to general background and advice for training purposes only, and is given solely on the understanding (which is deemed to be accepted by all who address or mark their messages to HELPMAIL) that neither the author nor Negotiate Ltd will be liable for any outcomes that may arise from that advice or from its execution by the recipient.

APPENDIX 2:

PART I: SCENARIO PRACTICE TEST

Millicent has been seconded to a committee charged with changing the remuneration package operating in a large organisation. Her expertise is in administration, not remuneration systems. She wants to make an impact on her career prospects by ensuring that the committee succeeds in its tasks. Her secondment was prompted by the Managing Executive realising that the remuneration project was making little progress and that further delays would make it impossible to modernise the pay system within the current tax year. The Chief Executive told her when she was advised of her secondment: 'The committee is moribund and I expect you to wake them up and get the project moving again.' He also added that she was not to be intimidated by the people on the committee who were more senior than her, including the director of personnel and the deputy finance director.

The next meeting of the seven-person committee was set for a date seven days away. It had been meeting every fourth Friday afternoon for five months, though not every member had attended all of the meetings (and there had been three replacements of personnel, including the project leader, during that time).

Millicent understood that there were several papers, memos and minutes of meetings in existence but she was not sure who had the copies. She knew the current project leader by sight but not well and she knew three other members of the committee from previous contact, but she did not know anything about the remaining three members, other than by their names, departments and phone extensions. She is keen to get started on her secondment, which she has to work around her administrative job (managing the organisation's database).

Millicent has asked you to advise her on how she might proceed to make her mark on the remuneration committee. Her questions to you are:

1. What is the first thing I should do?
2. Should I ask for copies of the committee's papers and minutes at the meeting?
3. Which, if any, members of the committee should I call before the meeting or should I wait to introduce myself at the meeting?
4. What should I do about not knowing anything about remuneration systems?
5. How might I get the committee moving as the Chief Executive wants? Should I 'hit the ground running' or take it more slowly?

PART II: ESSAY QUESTIONS

1. How might FAME help an influencing project?
2. Why does encouraging wallowing make a difference?
3. Why does one bad turn deserve another?

Please note that additional practice questions may be found on our web site at:
<www.negotiate.co.uk>

For assessment and comment on your answers, please post them to:

212

Gavin Kennedy
99 Caiyside
Edinburgh
EH10 7HR
Scotland
UK

or you may e-mail your answers to:
<gavin@negotiate.demon.co.uk>

Note: Please send a self-addressed envelope large enough to return your answers, plus either British postage stamps (for readers resident in the UK) or International Postal Coupon (for readers elsewhere) equivalent to the same amount it cost you to send your material to me. Allow up to 28 days for my response (I am often away on business).